AM I MY BROTHER'S KEEPER?

A book for the thinking Christian. It points a revealing finger at every layman and church leader who puts doctrine before the leading of the Holy Spirit, and explodes the myth of "doctrinal perfection." As a Christian who was "excommunicated" from his church because of his hunger for a "deeper walk" with God, Pat Boone shares his feelings about this painful experience and offers a wealth of scripture to show how God wants to unite us all in love.

AM I MY BROTHER'S KEEPER? Pat Boone's straight-talking bestseller about self-discovery —and God.

MY BROTHER'S KEEPER?

(ORIGINAL TITLE: *Dr. Balaam's Talking Mule*)

Pat Boone

PILLAR BOOKS NEW YORK

MY BROTHER'S KEEPER?
(Original title: *Dr. Balaam's Talking Mule*)

A PILLAR BOOK
Published by arrangement with Bible Voice, Inc.

Pillar Books edition published July, 1975

ISBN: 0—89129—028—1

Library of Congress Catalog Card Number: 75—7829

Printed in the United States of America

PILLAR BOOKS is a Division of Pyramid Publications,
919 Third Avenue, New York, New York 10022, U.S.A.

TABLE OF CONTENTS

To J. D. Bales,

my brother,

and

To a man named Richard Nixon,

a man, like me ...

who is, above and beyond all

other things, my brother

in Jesus

"Honor all men.

Love the brotherhood.

Fear God.

Honor the king."

I Peter 2:17

For Helen Kooiman Hosier

—a beautiful and fragrant bouquet;

Her loving editorial work

gave form to the substance.

Christ's into perfection. We are told that "all have sinned and come short of the glory of God" (verse 23)

PREFACE

This book is offered to my brother, whoever and wherever he is.

It grew out of correspondence with a lot of my brethren over the past several years, and I hoped through this one mind-busting effort to answer most of the major questions they've asked me, and challenges they've tossed me. Since *A New Song* I've really been bombarded by earnest Christians, especially conservative and evangelical ministers, theologians and teachers. I've been called variously a "heretic," a "mystic," a "wolf in sheep's clothing," a "spiritual Typhoid Mary," a doctrinal "lame brain," a "deceiver," "misled and misguided and misinformed," and some worse things. Yes, some worse things.

It's really been amazing. Here I am, just a working entertainer with a family, a regular churchgoer, a happy man who has experienced some wonderful miracles at the hand of God, who wants to share his happy discoveries with others; so I wrote a book about them.

And the fur began to fly!

The first thing that happened was that my family and I were asked out of our church—we call it "disfellowshipped." It was a sad and painful experience, though more for our elders and fellow-members than for us. See, we were nurtured and comforted by the precious indwelling Holy Spirit; we knew what we had, by experience. But our elders were convinced we were mistaken —we *had* to be mistaken, because their doctrine said so! We *couldn't* have experienced miracles, or the gifts of the Holy Spirit, or *any*thing supernatural; we just "thought" we had. Oh, sure, all those things you read about in the Bible happened, alright; but that was "back then," and just to "confirm the Word," and now those things "just don't happen."

In one of many, many meetings with the elders at our congregation, in their efforts to "straighten me out," one dear brother said to me, "Pat, we see the new love and commitment and devotion and enthusiasm in your life, and in Shirley's, and in your daughters'. That's all wonderful—we don't want to rob you of that.

"If it just wasn't mixed up with this 'Holy Spirit bit!'"

I had to chuckle and to respond this way, "What you're saying is that you like the *fruit* you see—but you want me to get that *tree* out of my back yard! Brother, it can't be done."

And so, eventually, in some tears, we parted company. Those dear men had agonized over the matter for months; they were our friends, and still are. They were *our* elders, and they felt it their anguished duty to separate us from the flock, for our good and to protect the rest of the congregation and to "defend the faith." I love them all the more for their willingness to pay a painful price for their convictions, to do their duty as they saw it. They did what they felt they had to do, as Christians, as elders, and as my brothers.

And that's the reason for this book.

I love those men—and they're my brothers.

I and my family haven't disfellowshipped anybody, especially men and women who call Jesus Savior and Lord. We don't feel a barrier between ourselves and those dear folks who inhabit and make up our church home of over ten years—they're still our brothers and sisters in the Lord, and we believe Romans 8:28 is still operative in their lives and in ours.

Didn't Paul and Barnabas, each filled with the Holy Spirit, have a disagreement, a "contention," so sharp that they split up and went their separate ways (Acts

15)? Did they cease to be brothers? Didn't the Lord go with each of them, and continue to work intimately with them?

Peter had *his* differences with Paul, too. Galatians 2:11 begins an account of an embarrassing "show-down" between the two spiritual giants. Yet Peter later had a warm and wonderful thing to say about "our beloved brother Paul" at the very end of his second letter to the church at large.

That's brotherhood!

That's what the apostle of love, the beloved John, was getting at in his epistles when he defined the basis of brotherhood (I John 5:1) and the practice of brotherhood (I John 3:11-24). In fact, he went so far as to say that because our elder brother Jesus laid down his life for us, we "ought to lay down our lives for the brethren"! That's a hard saying, isn't it?

Jesus, in the very shadow of the cross, prayed to His Father that we might all be one. Instead, we remain divided, and very self righteously so. Most Christians are self-appointed judges of others, right in the teeth of John's admonitions, Paul's dire warnings ("Thou art *inexcusable*, O man, whosoever thou art that judgest," Romans 2:1), and Jesus' own words in the Sermon on the Mount—"Judge not, *that you be not judged*" Matthew 7:1. And all these passages are directed at brothers!

Well, my brothers, a lot of them—especially the trained doctrinal experts—felt they had to judge me anyway. And one of the most often-repeated charges has been, "You say you're filled with the Holy Spirit, that you've spoken in tongues. You say you and your family have experienced some of the supernatural gifts of the Spirit, and miracles in answer to your prayers. Then how come you've made this mistake, or another? If the Holy Spirit is really directing and filling your life, why aren't you perfect in doctrine and manner of life and why don't you heal so-and-so and work this or that miracle?"

Well, I am afraid that I am a lot like Balaam's Ass. In Numbers 22 there's the wonderful story of the

11

prophet Balaam, a man with all the right theological credentials and ordination papers and on-the-job experience, who set out to curse or prophesy against the people of Israel. He felt he had good reasons, and his personal motives really blinded him to what God wanted him to do. He, as a religious leader, was determined to have things his way—regardless of the consequences. So he "saddled his ass" and went.

The Lord said "Okay, Balaam, have your way . . ." and then set an angel with a drawn sword in his path on the road, to destroy the prophet!

The dumb ass that Balaam was riding saw the angel in the road—and stopped. She could tell that to proceed any further on that course, resisting God, would be disastrous—but Dr. Balaam, the head of the religion department, was determined to go on, so he began to beat the poor animal mercilessly. How dare this uneducated brute refuse his directions!

After some considerable punishment, the ass collapsed under Balaam's weight, and still seeing the angel of God, began to *speak* to Balaam—*under the anointing of the Holy Spirit!* This barnyard animal was experiencing a gift from the Holy Spirit, a supernatural channel of communication, in which she asked the man of God why in the world he was being so harsh with her. Dr. Balaam replied, interestingly, "Because thou hast mocked me"; evidently his ego was bruised and his own pride damaged by the seeming independence of this inferior creature. And he added, "If I only had a sword, I'd kill you!"

Get this: the poor animal, probably four times heavier and stronger, speaking in soft, well modulated language—to the holy man, so enraged over the apparent rebellion of this ass that he was ready to lash out in violence! And the prophet's anger was so great that *he didn't seem to take notice of the miracle he was involved in.* Is it possible that anything like that could happen today?

So heated was the turmoil of the moment that the prophet and his ass even switched roles! The animal asked, speaking as the Spirit gave utterance (Acts 2),

12

"Have I ever behaved this way before . . ." And the man of God, like a barnyard beast, answered—"Nay."

Isn't that rich? The ass prophesying while the prophet brays!

How the angel kept a straight face, I don't know.

Maybe it's because the angels of God see this kind of spiritual role-swapping as the handiwork of the Devil —which it is. The prophet saw the ass as a rebel, because he was resisting the prophet's blind leading; when, in reality, the *prophet* was the real rebel, resisting God Himself! The angel revealed himself to Balaam and told him that this dumb brute he'd been beating had just saved the prophet's life—because, in that instance, the ass had been more sensitive to the Spirit than the prophet!

Now please don't misunderstand: I'm not using this story to "put down" all theologians and to exalt barnyard prophets like myself. I'm simply pleading that we stay open-minded and open-hearted, receptive to insights from brothers in Christ, regardless of their credentials! I've been blessed by God through firemen and fishermen, preachers and politicians, wise men and widows—Jesus promises surprises to those born of the Spirit (John 3:8)!!

Oh, the Lord has done some strange and marvelous things—and it's still His way.

Over and over through the centuries, in a still small voice or thundering from the heavens, through messengers, or scriptures, or in personal encounters, in thousands of ways, our Father has demanded, I WILL BE BELIEVED!

And he demands the same thing today.

After this incredible eye-opening encounter, the prophet Balaam went on to far greater service in his Godly office than ever, surrendering to the Holy Spirit even though his physical life was threatened—and uttering magnificent prophecy under the anointing of God, even speaking one of the first specific references to a Messiah, a Star who would rise out of Jacob to assume dominion. See, Romans 8:28 was operating even back then!

13

What they went through together, the prophet and the ass, wound up being a blessing for both of them—and for all God's people!

I believe my brother the mule can teach us something valuable today, if we will listen.

This book is about a lot of other, dynamic, beautiful, and necessary things that we've allowed Satan to wrest from our grasp. Like relationship with God on a personal, day-to-day basis, like miraculous dimension in our lives, like the supernatural guidance and gifts of the Holy Spirit—and like brotherhood.

Isn't it terribly significant that *the world's first two brothers,* Cain and Abel, divided over religious matters? And that the world's first bloody murder was committed in anger kindled by spiritual jealousy? Have we really come very far from Eden?

The Lord makes it very clear, both in Genesis 4 and I John 3:12, that it was *not the difference in their religious sacrifices* that caused Him to reject Cain's offering; it was the unrighteousness in Cain's *life!* And Paul, in Hebrews 11, adds that Abel's sacrifice was mixed with real *faith,* where Cain's evidently wasn't. Still smoldering and wrathful, smarting from the Lord's reprimand, perhaps feeling intimidated by his brother's apparent "pipeline to God"—Cain bludgeoned his own brother to death. Like Balaam would have slain the ass. Like Esau would have slain Jacob, and his brothers would have slain Joseph.

Like we would crucify Jesus.

Oh, you don't think we would? Are we really so different from the Pharisee and the Sadducee, the intolerant religious people of His day, who tried every way they could to explain away His miracles and His mysterious teaching, even suggesting that His power probably came from the devil? Don't we feel a malicious, vengeful feeling stir deep within us when somebody dares suggest that we, like the Sadducees Jesus accused in Matthew 22, "do err, not knowing the scriptures, *nor the power of God*"? Boy, I've felt some of that venom in *me;* and I've felt a lot of it directed *at* me from brethren, when I've talked openly about our new

14

commitment to Jesus, and His manifestations in our lives. There is some of what slew Jesus in every one of us!

What was it our Saviour said, in His very first sermon? "Whosoever is angry with his brother without a cause shall be in danger of the judgment: and whosoever shall say to his brother 'Vain fellow,' shall be in danger of the council: but whosoever shall say, 'Thou fool,' shall be in danger of hell fire. . . .

Therefore, if thou bring thy gift to the altar, and there rememberest that thy brother hath ought against thee;

Leave there thy gift before the altar, and go thy way; first be reconciled to thy brother, and then come and offer thy gift." (Matt. 5:22-4)

I want to be reconciled to my brothers and sisters. I AM MY BROTHER'S KEEPER.

And he is mine.

I'm learning how to worship my Lord in Spirit and in truth, and I want to raise my hands to Jesus, with my brother at my side. Very shortly, I feel, we'll all be kneeling before the God of Heaven and earth and confessing the name of Jesus, seeing Him face to face. And He, by His Spirit, is calling us together, to be reconciled before His altar.

He pleads with us to "Submit to one another in the fear of God" and to "in honor prefer one another," for our own sakes and for Jesus' sake.

There's not much time left. He wants to join the various parts of His believing body together, the knees, knuckles and noses, as well as the more lovely and presentable parts. If any of us have placed our faith in Jesus, then we are being added to His body, and He wants to bring us into the unity of the Spirit, to instruct and perfect us into one vital, dynamic and diverse organism, "unto a perfect man, unto the measure of the stature of the fullness of Christ!"

It's to this end that I offer this book. It's the hopeful effort of a childlike Christian, an apprentice ass, to share the mercies and miracles of God with my brothers and sisters, many of whom are much farther along

15

in their own walks with God than I am. But as they have blessed me, I hope to offer some blessing to them.

And to you.

I devoutly pray that the Lord will favor me, as He did that other dumb animal, and give me something, by the anointing of His Spirit, to share with Balaam my brother.

"Now God Himself and our Father, and our Lord Jesus Christ, direct our way unto you.

And the Lord make you to increase and abound in love one toward another, and *toward all men,* even as we do toward you:

To the end He may establish your hearts unblameable in holiness before God, even our Father, at the coming of our Lord Jesus Christ—with *all* His saints." (I Thess. 3:11-13)

1

A GOD'S EYE VIEW OF THINGS

As I write this, I'm looking down at the Earth from around 35,000 feet, flying across country. It's a beautiful place to be, and the view seems especially clear, both physically and spiritually.

I love to fly, and I love to think, and the two seem to mesh so well. Perhaps a man gets just a little closer to a God's eye view of things from up here, or at least a little better spiritual perspective.

I've often envied Moses his forty years in the wilderness; *that wasn't wasted time*—It was during this time that he had precious communion with God, preparation of the highest sort for what God had for him to do. When he came back into Egypt, he was trained to see things from God's point of view, not man's. And though he was still human, and he sinned, his percentage was unusually high. He was made strong—not physically or intellectually, but spiritually—by his long communion with God.

As I fly, I'm always newly impressed with the truth that each little winking light, each rooftop, each office window, each tiny moving car, each farm and little fenced yard represents a separate world of existence for somebody. Each represents a unique chain of experience, an eternally different stamped, shaped and molded personality, a separate relationship to God. I'll never see those peoples' faces in this life, but God knows their heartbeats, their thoughts, their hopes and dreams, faults and strengths, failures and little triumphs.

And He died for each of those myriads of people down there, just as He did for me up here.

We're not a seething mass to Him; we're not a teeming herd of humankind, to be rounded up, corralled, branded and dipped, inventoried and turned out to pasture. We're *individuals* to Him, isolated in the universe, created specifically for an intimate personal relationship with our Father.

And God sees us, knows us, hears us where we are. This is a precious fact about Jesus: God in human form. He saw and confronted people where He found them, and He knew them individually. When Nicodemus came to see Him by night, Jesus concentrated totally on him, and addressed Himself to his concerns. The rich young ruler experienced the same thing, as did Zacchaeus, and Lazarus, and each of his disciples. He met them *where they were,* and began his relationship with them there. His response to them was governed by their needs, questions and actions, as He alone could know them. He met all kinds of people, but He didn't treat them all the same.

The Samaritan woman taken in adultery experienced His mercy. The Pharisees received His condemnation, and the moneychangers His anger.

In Matthew, in less than ten verses, Jesus blessed Peter for speaking truth revealed to him by God, and also severely rebuked him for allowing himself to be influenced by Satan. *He knows us* individually, minute by minute, and meets us *where we are,* and will lead us, if we let Him, to where He wants us to be!

Only God can do this. No man is capable of it—we don't have a God's eye view of things! But we try, don't we? Oh, how we try!

What is it, really, that we are doing?

2

THE HAZARDS OF PLAYING
DEPUTY SHEPHERD

I have had to learn the hard way the folly and futility
of trying to judge other people by my own limited understanding. I have heard many other people make this
same admission.

Often we make the mistake of trying to herd people
together, like cattle. We try to jerk them from where
they are to where *we* are, or, to where *we* believe
Christ is, and where *we* believe He wants them to be.
Instead we should be encouraging them to meet Jesus
where they are, and allow Him to lead them individually. We're afraid that if we just leave it to them and
Jesus, they won't hear Him, they'll misread His leading,
they won't be acceptable to Him—they won't follow as
well as we do!

Our concern is good as it springs from love. Our in-
tentions are honorable but they're human, like Peter's
in Matthew 16:22. Let me refresh your memory. In
that verse and in preceding verses, we see Jesus speaking plainly to His disciples "about going to Jerusalem,
and what would happen to Him there—that He would
suffer at the hands of the Jewish leaders, that He would
be killed, and that three days later He would be raised
to life again" (verse 21). There we see Peter taking
Jesus aside to remonstrate with him. "Heaven forbid,
sir," he said, "This is not going to happen to you!"

Jesus turned on Peter and said, "Get away from me, you Satan! You are a dangerous trap to me. You are thinking merely from a human point of view, and not from God's" (verses 22,23 *The Living Bible*).

How like Peter we are! But we cannot know people "where they are," or know them as Jesus knows them. Our function, I believe, should be to imitate the Apostle Andrew in John I, and simply endeavor to introduce our brother to Jesus, as Andrew did Peter, and then let Jesus lead him from there.

Of course, whatever help we can offer, whatever thought and experience we can share, whatever exhortation—and more important than all the rest put together, whatever *example* of Jesus *in* us we can demonstrate—we should gladly do it. But beyond that, when we start judging where a man is in his relationship to Christ and start trying to become spiritual "Deputy Shepherds," with self-made badges, handcuffs and warrants, we play right into the hands of the devil, from whom comes all strife, bitterness and division.

How the devil loves it when we start judging each other and deciding who is and who isn't acceptable in the kingdom of heaven! That's *his* ball game! After all, his original sin according to Isaiah 14, was deciding "I will be like the most High." In daring to aspire to a place of equality with God, Lucifer was "brought down to hell, to the sides of the pit" (verse 15). How we need to remind ourselves that it was the original temptation of man to have the knowledge of good and evil, *to be like God,* which brought about Adam's fall.

We're too small to play in the devil's ball game—we are not his equal, but he persuades us to try; why, he even convinces us that *it's our duty*.

And so, with all good conscience, and motivated much like Peter, thinking to protect Christ and His body and His truth—as if He hadn't demonstrated His divine ability to do that Himself for two thousand years —we find brethren criticizing, judging, suspecting, condemning, binding, threatening and rejecting each other in the name of the Lord. We lose confidence in His ability to lead His sheep, and we start trying to do

20

it for Him, and become "the blind leading the blind." It's pitiful to experience or to see.

The hazards of playing "Deputy Shepherd" are too high. I, for one, would rather be just one of His sheep.

3

JESUS IS OUR INFALLIBLE SHEPHERD

The Christian life is an exciting journey, and Jesus is our infallible Shepherd.

He knows the weaknesses of our intellects and our limited understanding, and can be trusted to fill in all the gaps and lead us gently and surely as we completely surrender our will to Him. This is tough, because we keep wanting to hang on to our own understanding and traditional doctrine—our preconceived views, sometimes handed down to us from generation to generation.

In fact, we dumb humans often confuse the "gospel" with our own "doctrine." They are not necessarily—or even very often—the same. But Jesus, through His Word and by His Spirit will lead us individually into understanding the truth of His Word.

If I understand what I've read about church history over the last two thousand years, truth has come to light and the church flourished *not* when it was rigidly enforced, policed, dictated and intellectually regulated by men—but precisely when earnest men rebelled *against* just that kind of religion, and sought the right for each individual to stand before God alone and independent.

I myself grew up in a background governed by a rigid set of rules and a "black and white" understanding of the Scriptures according to our church doctrine, which automatically placed anyone who didn't see it our way *outside the body of Christ*.

I was so uncomfortable many times, and so troubled as I saw other people who may not have worn the same "church" name or worshipped in quite the same way as I, but they had such love and joy, and sometimes a radiance that indicated a real and vital relationship with Jesus. Many times they seemed to have more than I did! I confess that I couldn't understand it.

This caused me to do some deep soul searching. As I did, I began to see some of my Christian brothers and sisters in a new light—as fellow seekers and fellow servants.

Now, that doesn't mean I condone error that I may grow spiritually (according to my understanding of God's Word), but it does mean that I am depending more and more on the Holy Spirit to bring us together —and not so much on my own reasoning, rhetoric or intellect. I have come to realize that I've got so much error in my own life; how can I possibly judge or condemn my brother or sister because of the error I think I can see in his or her life? Can one confessed failure (as every Christian must be) condemn another?

There's such joy and freedom in this outlook!

It relieves you of the burden of judging another's relationship with Christ. It puts the emphasis back on your own service and yieldedness, and gives you greater love and compassion for others. I have since discovered that through prayer and study and fellowship with people who may have different views than mine, God can do a wondrous thing. By His Spirit, working through our love, He can actually help us *each* to see His truth and His will more perfectly! Life has really gotten exciting, as a result, in the last couple of years for us in the Boone family.

The Holy Spirit will guide, teach, instruct, comfort and give a man great joy—but He won't make you a robot or a transistor saint! Just as he did with Peter in Matthew 16, Satan will try to use our strengths *and* our weaknesses—but so will God if we turn them all over to Him. By His greater power, He will work all things together for our good, if we let Him, and love Him.

This brings me back to my starting point, our precious Lord meets us where we are, and just as we are. We should be prepared to meet Him, *and each other,* in the same way.

None of us is perfect, and all of us sin.

4

PROGRAMMED BY GOD'S OWN SPIRIT

Jesus says, "I stand at the door and knock; if *any* man will open, I will come in . . ."

You can't pry that door open for anybody, nor can I. You can't *close* it for anybody, either denying the Lord's entrance, nor can I. And you can't be in there, knowing what's going on between a man and his Lord, nor can I.

Paul, writing Timothy (I Timothy 3:16), speaks of the "mystery of godliness." And it is a mystery, a personal and spiritual mystery. We can't really understand or comprehend it. Paul says that it is *"with the heart that man believeth unto righteousness!"* (Romans 10:10) How can a man believe with his heart? I think I know now, at least in part, because I've had this experience. There was a time, however, when I didn't fully understand what "heart belief" meant.

The two most powerful motivators of man are *fear* and *faith*. Where do you feel fear? In your brain? No, you may understand why you should be afraid intellectually, but unless you *feel* fear, it's not likely to motivate you much.

On the other hand, you can intellectually believe (even the devils do) and still not be motivated to real righteousness. Until you believe with your *heart*, until you *feel* with your faith, through encounter and experience, it won't motivate you to real righteousness.

As humans, we keep going at things backwards. We keep trying to approach Christ, and serve Him, intellectually—like our brother Nicodemus. Remember him in the third chapter of John's gospel? As Jesus spoke to him of the necessity of regeneration—of being born again—Nicodemus kept muttering, "How can these things be?"

We need to put our hands into His, and fall to our knees exclaiming, *"My Lord and my God!"* We need personal encounters and intimate experiences, like Paul's and Peter's, and those other first-century Christians. We need simply to open the door of our hearts and let Jesus come in, as He promised He would.

It's then that these wonderful, though still pitifully human brains of ours can really work for us—programmed by God's own Spirit, with the Scriptures bursting to life before our very eyes and in our daily experience!

To try it in the reverse order is like trying to manually operate a big computer—we may get something done, but not nearly what God intended. He gave us these personal computers for a reason, *His* reason. He meant us to plug into the same eternal current that framed the universe and inspired His Scripture. Only then will our brains serve us properly.

How we need His Spirit to guide us in this rapidly crumbling, chaotic world we're clinging to!

There is a whole lot of confusion, though, about the fullness and indwelling of the Holy Spirit; particularly about the ones who indicate that they've received some supernatural gift or manifestation of that indwelling spirit.

There are those who think that all "charismatics" should automatically be infallible and above sin and incapable of any kind of mistake. And yet we read in the Bible that Peter and Paul and all the disciples—and certainly the church at Corinth—*though filled with the Spirit,* were all capable of error and did make many mistakes.

Should we expect more of a Spirit-filled Christian today than Peter, Paul or these others could manage?

26

5

WHO ARE **YOU** TO CRITICIZE GOD?

The fullness of the Holy Spirit and the accompanying gifts were *never* a guarantee of infallibility. I feel like this should be on a giant billboard in Times Square! So many people have the tragic misconception that a truly "spirit filled" person, should be incapable of error.

It ain't so—and never was!

The fullness of the Holy Spirit and the accompanying gifts were, however, a guarantee of greater power to witness; (Acts 1:8) of justification and freedom in Christ (Romans 8:24-27); of deep kinship with God (Romans 8:14-17); of much more perfect understanding of God's Word and Will; (I Corinthians 2:10-16); of wonderful spiritual edification, both individually and collectively (I Corinthians 14); of the certainty of our inheritance from God (Ephesians 1:13-14); of the very presence of God dwelling in us (I John 3:23-24); and of greater capacity to love and serve and sense so many other wonderful treasures.

I and my family—and so many others—have experienced these things in greater measure. But we're *not* infallible and, of course, we make mistakes. This can be very, very humbling, and God allows it, since he never wanted robots. Then, when we recognize our own failings and mistakes, acknowledging them before Him and others, calling upon Him to direct our thinking, we continue to experience the infusion of His

27

mighty power working on our behalf. James says to spirit-filled believers, "confess your faults to one another"! and when we do that, it cleanses us and shows to those who are watching us so carefully, that any error that creeps into our writing or talking is strictly human error.

Every day, God's kids should get into the Word, calling upon the Holy Spirit to redirect our thinking as we confess our own inadequacy.

In Psalm ninety-six, David exhorts us to "Sing a new song to the Lord! Sing it everywhere around the world! Sing out his praises! Bless his name. Each day tell someone that he saves."

"Publish his glorious acts throughout the earth. Tell everyone about the amazing things he does. For the Lord is great beyond description, and greatly to be praised. . . . Give him the glory he deserves!" (Psalm 96:1-4a, 8 *The Living Bible*).

God isn't new, nor the singer—but the song of praise should be *ever* new, tingling with fresh discovery of God's greatness, His power and His mercy, His nearness and His love, the wonder and accuracy of His Work!

For years, I sang to God out of habit and duty, with a rather vague hope that it mattered to Him somehow. I thought I knew our Father about as well as human beings *could* know him, and all sense of discovery was gone. Nothing remained but the grim duties of stubborn faith and studying "to show myself approved unto God." I wondered if I could make it!

I couldn't.

I failed, and failed miserably. And thank God I did! Because out of my failure and frustration, has come a wonderful "new" discovery—and Jesus said it bluntly in John 14, "I am the way, the truth, and the life: no man cometh unto the Father, but by me"! (John 14:6). I can come to God only through a personal *relationship* with Jesus!

The study of the Bible and obedience are essential and good, but only that daily, individual relationship brings the kind of joy that spills over in "a new song."

The question is frequently asked, "What's happened to the Boones?" It is asked mainly because of the experiences my wife, Shirley, and I have related in books, correspondence, and the witness we have been able to give wherever we go.

Actually, we haven't "gone" *anything* except Christian—100%. By this I don't mean to imply that we're special, or better than anybody else. In fact we're admitting that we've been failures on our own, and that we've had to just surrender totally to Jesus, and commit ourselves—our very all—to Him. Out of this total surrender has come my "new song!" I've tried to do, as I felt led by the Holy Spirit, what David suggested in Psalm 96 and 98; to bless His name with a song.

Our God is an infinitely versatile Father. I'll never cease to be amazed at the many different ways He deals with His children. But always, no matter where or how He meets us, His purpose is to draw us closer to Himself. Jesus went in and got down with "publicans and sinners," the mafioso, the prostitutes and profiteers of His day. And while the religious hierarchy stood off and gnashed their teeth, Jesus was quietly transforming lives! And these crooks and "undesirables," changed from within, went running to their friends shouting, "Come and see!"

I think this is what the psalmist meant when he urged us to sing out his praises and publish his glorious acts throughout the earth. We should *all* be writing books and songs about the miracles in our lives! And when something starts to happen to you—you will!

I praise God that He chooses to use us human, fallible, struggling Christians with motes *and* beams in our eyes. Sometimes we may use words incorrectly, but we do know that *something* has happened to us!

In Romans 9, we see the Apostle Paul expressing deep concern and sorrow for his kinsmen the Jews. He cries out with anguish of heart as he affirms that his own life is centered "in Christ" and that his "conscience" is under the direct influence of "the Holy Spirit." Paul, don't forget, was himself a Jew, by nature very legalistic and at one time bent on *destroying every*

29

vestige of Christianity—until he was remarkably over-powered by the Holy Spirit on the road to Damascus.

Now, as he pleads with his Jewish brothers, Paul demands, *"Who are you to criticize God?"* (Romans 9:20 *The Living Bible*).

Right on, Brother Paul—right on.

If we could only stand on the mountain top of history and look back at our day—right now—as we can Paul's day, we'd be able to see more clearly how God is working intimately, ingeniously, in every stream of humanity. We'd see Him waiting in the Damascus roads of countless individuals, revealing Himself in every unique way, drawing all of us together and offering us His Spirit, "so that everyone can see how very great his glory is" (Romans 9:22-24, Author's paraphrase and *The Living Bible*).

6

CONCESSIONS THAT OPEN DOORS OF FELLOWSHIP

You don't pick oranges in Iowa.

Just so, you and I are the products of the environment in which we were raised. Right? But—there's a very important difference. We aren't orange trees.

We have minds—and wills—and spirits. We can *change!* And that's the business God is in: people changing.

To do that, He often uproots us. Takes us out of our natural environment and plants us in strange soil.

But, oh, how we hate to change!

Our loving Father knows what a traumatic thing it is to feel our roots slipping out of familiar ground, to feel a possible transplant coming on. Oh, how we want the world to stay as we always thought it was, and to know that even when we wander away from God, we can come back and find Him waiting patiently in the church of our childhood. What a shock to find Him instead, waiting for us *outside* the church—in our wilderness road!

Like a Heavenly Highwayman, He may kidnap us and never let us go "home" again!

Many young people today rebel against blind tradition and step out of the church in which they grew up —throwing aside all they've been taught, with a total rejection of Christ and His teachings. Others, restless

31

and hungry for real spiritual food, search the scriptures with more diligence. They read about things they've never experienced—and their quest for more of the things of God may lead them beyond the home church door. They're not rebelling (though they may be accused of that) but they are simply studying, searching, learning and growing.

Have such as these "left the faith," or "departed from sound doctrine"? The answer to that, of course, depends upon where their search for things spiritual has led them. If, in their wanderings, they follow some new god, some other authority than the Bible, the answer is *yes*. But when that search is grounded in the Word of God, and where there is scriptural evidence to support their beliefs, and they still hold to the essential doctrines of faith, repentance, confession of sins, baptism, and all the other teachings of Jesus, we must carefully weigh our answer. Are such as these to be "disfellowshipped" from the church, the body of believers?

Well, it happens, dear friend—it happens. All over this country—a nation founded on individual religious liberty—many churches, in their anxiety to protect what they believe to be their doctrinal purity, are "disfellowshipping" believers who have shown an interest in deeper spirituality, especially when there is an accompanying experience related to one of the gifts of the spirit, namely speaking in tongues.

And if while studying and searching and experiencing new things with God, the earnest Spirit-filled believer begins to share his discoveries with his own church folks he may be branded a "wolf in sheep's clothing" and a "deceiver"! He may have been told he should have "come out in the open" and have "made a stand" rather than quietly sharing with a few who seem especially interested.

Was the Apostle Paul being deceptive when he fellowshipped with those who didn't eat meat offered to idols? Should he have told them that he *did* eat meat? Should he have "made a stand?" No, he knew Christian fellowship was bigger than that—there was no reason to make an issue of their doctrinal differences.

Was he being deceptive when he shaved his head, according to Jewish custom, after he'd taught so forcefully *against* the necessity of such things for the Christian? No, Paul was not a deceiver—he simply made a harmless concession to open a door of fellowship that otherwise would have been denied him.

But at the same time, I'm sure Paul didn't take that vow lightly; it was a deeply personal, subjective experience of devotion and purification.

This, I believe, is the key to "what's happening to the Boones" and many other believers. We've had deeply personal, subjective experiences with God, in praise and devotion. But, we have not sought to bind these personal experiences on others, nor will we. *We have sought to lift up Christ,* not our personal experience; and yet, when we've been asked about our experiences, we've shared them. It's almost impossible to share the fruits of the Spirit without revealing their source. Is this deception?

Now, I'm sure that in many instances, my own experience included, our zeal is mixed with human failing. How we need to pray, asking God to overrule, and that in spite of us the sum total will be good. We love Him so much, we love His Word and His Church, and we've rededicated our lives to His service. We've been snatched up by the Heavenly Highwayman and we joyously ride the wind with Him, singing His song. But still Paul's self-examination in I Corinthians 9:27 rings in my ears: "But I keep my body under, and bring it into subjection: lest that by any means, when I have preached to others, I myself should be a castaway."

The Apostle Paul recognized that we are so much the product of our environments, that we naturally resist the pain of change, and that because of early conditioning it may be very difficult to accept even the most eloquent, startling testimony from one who appears to challenge the "security" of our familiar ground. So, by maintaining kinship with the non-

Christians and the weak Christians, Paul had an open door through which to bring in the living Jesus.

Oh, that we would be door-openers—instead of fence-builders.

7

HAVE WE SETTLED FOR DOCTRINE?

Sometimes I think we forget that Jesus and the Apostle Paul went into the homes of publicans and sinners, ate with them, were welcome in their company, were criticized for it, but still went into the synagogues and even worshipped with the Jews.

I have already alluded to the fact that Paul, who was so tough on Judaism (enforcing Jewish laws on Christians), went into the temple and shaved his head. This was a very serious Jewish vow. And, of course, the New Testament often spotlights Jesus fellowshipping with those who were looked down upon and scorned by the religious leaders of His day.

On the other hand, Jesus also made it a point to converse with the Pharisees when they tried to trip him up on some theological issue, and He could also be found in the Temple worshipping. Neither Jesus nor Paul feared their critics or the scoffers.

The Church today has a long way to go to meet the standard set by Jesus' example. The Apostle Paul boldly followed the precedent Jesus set, and so did the other disciples. How we, as 20th Century followers of our Lord, can ignore the written record of His footsteps is very difficult for me to understand.

We have so often been afraid of being affected or stained by those who don't share all of our doctrinal beliefs, that we have failed to be the salt of the earth;

35

therefore, when I *do* hear from or read about those who are following the Holy Spirit's leading, I get what I call "spiritual goose bumps."

I earnestly believe that many theologians and preachers have "put the Spirit aside until He doesn't dwell in the Church like He once did." I recall the story of the old evangelist named Follette, who was so close to the Lord. He told of going to church service one day and found it beautiful, ordered, artistic and perfectly performed in every detail. About midway through the service he says he could almost vow that the Lord nudged him and whispered, "Come on, let's you and I get out of here—they don't need us."

It appears that in much of Christendom today, *we have settled for form and doctrine* instead of the living Spirit of God and His continuing work and leading in our lives. We keep referring to the "all sufficiency" of the scriptures; by that we seem to mean that the Bible is sufficient as it sits on a shelf or as we memorize certain passages of it and use those passages to convert people to our doctrine. It doesn't occur to us that the same Holy Spirit who inspired and wrote the Bible *still wants to write more chapters in our very lives!*

8

"IS THE CHURCH SPLIT OVER
DEEPER SPIRITUALITY?"

In II Corinthians 3, Paul writes that he doesn't want long letters of self-recommendation from the Corinthian Christians. "The only letter I need," he stresses, "is you yourselves! By looking at the good change in your hearts, everyone can see that we have done a good work among you. They can see that you are a letter from Christ, written by us. It is not a letter written with pen and ink, but by the *Spirit of the living God;* not one carved on stone, but in human hearts" (verses 2 and 3 *The Living Bible*).

Does that scripture shout at you like it does to me?

Once we feel the working of the Spirit in our own lives, we recognize the truth of what Paul is saying. It strikes home with startling impact! *The Holy Spirit isn't writing in ink anymore; He's writing in the lives of human beings*—at least the ones who are yielded to His authorship.

Well, write on, Holy Spirit, write on!

Most of us have just flatly disobeyed Paul's specific commands in I Thessalonians 5:19-20. There we are told to "Quench not the Spirit. Despise not prophesyings." That means we are not to smother the Holy Spirit; we are not to scoff at those who prophesy, but we are to test everything that is said to be sure it is true, and if it is, then accept it. And what is the standard by which we are to do that testing? Is it not the Bible?

I am deeply saddened to see that many of the brethren throughout Christendom are so vehement on the subject of the Holy Spirit and personal experiences with God through prayer, study and service, that they are demanding that sides be drawn. People are disfellowshipped from the Church, ministers are denounced, and earnest, Bible-believing Christians divided. All this, not because of unbelief, adultery or idolatry—all valid reasons, according to the Bible, for disfellowship; but because some have sought closer communion with God, and *have experienced things, which have deepened their dedication and devotion to the risen Christ.*

I cannot help but ask the question: Is the Church supposed to be split over deeper spirituality?

I cannot help but feel that if the Apostle Paul were in our midst today, he would instruct us exactly as he instructed the infant Church. He would tell us to be patient with each other; to pray for each other; to study and search the scriptures together. And then, I think Paul might give to us the same exhortation he gave to the Ephesian Christians:

"I pray that your hearts will be flooded with light so that you can see something of the future he has called you to share. I want you to realize that God has been made rich because we who are Christ's have been given to him!

I pray that you will begin to understand how incredibly great his power is to help those who believe him. It is that same mighty power that raised Christ from the dead and seated him in the place of honor at God's right hand in heaven, far, far above any other king or ruler or dictator or leader. Yes, his honor is far more glorious than that of anyone else in this world or in the world to come. And God has put all things under his feet and made him the supreme Head of the church —which is his body, filled with himself, the Author and Giver of everything everywhere" (Ephesians 1:17-23 *The Living Bible*).

9

JESUS, TORN IN PIECES

Does your Bible read like mine?

As I've been reading through my New Testament, it's become very obvious to me that among those Spirit-filled churches in the first century there were significant differences in belief, devotion, worship and service. Even Peter and Paul had their differences; and in Acts fifteen I read where apostles and elders had "much disputing" among them. In the thirty-ninth verse of that same chapter we find the contention was so sharp between Paul and Barnabas that they split up!

Paul recognized this human failing and it grieved his heart. He tackled the problem of division in several of his letters. Other writers of the New Testament also saw this for what it was—a devious, desperate scheme of the devil himself to divide the church. In most cases, the writers of these letters were addressing themselves, it appears, *to Spirit-filled Christians*. Was the Holy Spirit failing—or were they, the Christians, failing in their sensitivity to the leading of the Spirit?

In First Corinthians it's obvious that the church in Corinth, which had all the gifts of the Spirit operating in its midst, also had enormous sins among its members. They evidently made almost a drunken orgy of the Lord's Supper, and were divided into factions or "denominations."

Paul wrote: "Dear brothers, I beg you, in the name

of the Lord Jesus Christ, to stop arguing among yourselves. Let there be real harmony so that there won't be splits in the church. I plead with you to be of one mind, united in thought and purpose. Some of you are saying, 'I am a follower of Paul'; and others say that they are for Apollos or for Peter, and some that they alone are the true followers of Christ. And so, in effect, you have broken Christ into many pieces" (I Corinthians 1:10-13 *The Living Bible*).

The King James version asks the question, "Is Christ divided?" (verse 13). Paul's question echoes right down to today. The Answer, obviously, is "no—but His church is!" And it's divided precisely for the reason that each group thinks it has all the truth and is entirely correct, and that the others are wrong and somehow displeasing to God.

I like what N. B. Hardeman said long ago: "We don't claim to be the only Christians—but we do claim to be Christians *only*." That, it seems to me, is what Christians should be saying. *We all serve Christ imperfectly,* and yet we can make the claim that we are Christians. But it does grieve me to see believers meeting week after week, and year after year, and confronting the same problems all the time with no real solutions and no real power apparent in their lives.

The Apostle Paul, in writing to young Timothy, expressed concern over what was going to happen in the last days. One of the things mentioned has to do with churchgoers. Paul says they will have a form of godliness, but *deny the power* thereof (2 Timothy 3:5).

We have developed a terrible tendency, within the church, to confuse faith with doctrinal position and understanding.

The Apostle Paul, a brilliant and learned man, preached a very simple faith—and a complex doctrine. Inspired by the Holy Spirit, this brilliant man (who had an intense *personal experience* with Jesus himself) shows us the difference between faith and doctrine, or faith and law. In Romans 3, from the twentieth verse on to the end of the chapter, Paul makes it abundantly clear that God realized no one could keep His law, or

Christ's law, perfectly. We are told that we have *all* sinned and come short of the glory of God (verse 23).

It helps me immensely to zero in on the fact that Jesus is the Shepherd and He leads us all individually if we let Him. This doesn't mean that we'll always agree with each other—even on fundamental things. It *does* mean that we are all dependent upon the mercy and the grace of God for forgiveness and salvation. It *does* mean that though we differ on many things, we *can be* brothers and sisters in the Lord.

Christ *is not* divided—when our individual worshipful focus is on Him, and not each other's faults.

In the happiest family I know—the Boone family—there are six different individuals. We differ in a lot of ways, and in some areas we're as different as night and day. I'm still puzzled about the female reactions to many situations we face—and the girls can't figure me out, either. But you know what? Our love, our blood ties, our sense of interdependence, our mutual experiences—and the Holy Spirit we share—has molded us into a wonderful, glowing unit.

God meant His people, His church, to be just that: a family.

He *made* us different! And He *loves* our differences. He *wants* to deal with us as unique individuals. And yet, He *wants* us to be one, as a family is one.

Listen to His own heart-cry: "Behold, how good and how pleasant it is for brethren to dwell together in unity!.

It is like the precious ointment upon the head, that ran down upon the beard, even Aaron's beard, that went down to the skirts of his garments,

Like the dew of Hermon, and like the dew that descended upon the mountains of Zion; for there the Lord commanded the blessing, even life forevermore." (Psalm 133)

Solomon reminds us that among the *seven things that God hates* is "he that soweth discord among brethren"! Proverbs 6:16-19.

And finally Jesus Himself, in the anguish of the garden, in the very shadow of the cross: "Neither pray I

41

for these alone, but for them also who *shall* believe on me through their word;

That they all may be one, as thou, Father, art in me, and I in thee, that they also may be one in us; that the world may believe that thou hast sent me." (John 17)

10

TAKING THE LIMITS OFF GOD

When will we learn that there can be *diversity* within
the body of Christ, his church, without division.

It can only come as we individually take the limits
off God and yield our lives as completely as we can to
Him—and to the leading of His Spirit and His Word.

Those who have done this are staggered at the things
God can and will do with a yielded life. Incredible,
wonderful, miraculous, God-given things are happening in the lives of believers!

Even preachers!

Automatically, with yieldness, there comes the lib-
erating recognition that *we don't know all the answers,* and that we can't judge men's hearts or their
standings with God. *Only He can.*

If we're to move into a deeper walk with Jesus
through His Spirit, then rigid legalism has got to go.
*Each of us has to give up the judge's bench and move
down to a witness seat.* Then, as we open ourselves to
the leading and moving of the Holy Spirit, we can
count on it—God will bring us together, without any of
us compromising one valid scriptural principle. It's supernatural!

There were so many botch-ups hindering the power
and progress of Jesus' ministry in the early churches,
scattered as they were. This was a "new thing in the
Earth," after all, and people were still people, with all

their prides and prejudices and fleshly human hang-ups. Peter and Paul and James had to write lots of letters! How thankful we can be that the Holy Spirit moved their pens—and then miraculously kept some of these letters for us.

But a lot of us fail to realize those letters were written to *us,* too!

Just as if our names were inserted at the top of each one! And because we think we're reading "dead letters" we ignore a lot of the specific teaching.

In urging you and me (and *all* the readers of his letters) to pay attention to what he was saying, Paul reminds us "the Holy Spirit's power is in my words," proving that the message is from God. "I remind you of this," he states, "because *I want your faith to stand firmly upon God,* not on man's great ideas" (I Corinthians 2:4, 5 Author's paraphrase and *The Living Bible*).

With 20th Century immediacy, Paul explains: "This is what is meant by the Scriptures which say that no mere man has ever seen, heard or even imagined what wonderful things God has ready for those who love the Lord. But we know about these things because God has sent his Spirit to tell us all of God's deepest secrets. No one can really know what anyone else is thinking, or what he is really like, except that person himself. *And no one can know God's thoughts except God's own Spirit.* And God has actually given us his Spirit (not the world's spirit) to tell us about the wonderful free gifts of grace and blessing that God has given us. In telling you about these gifts we have even used the very words given to us by the Holy Spirit, not words that we as men might choose. So we use the Holy Spirit's words to explain the Holy Spirit's facts. But the man who isn't a Christian can't understand and can't accept these thoughts from God, which the Holy Spirit teaches us. They sound foolish to him, because *only those who have the Holy Spirit within them can understand what the Holy Spirit means. Others just can't take it in.* But the spiritual man has insight into everything, and that bothers and baffles the man of the world, who can't understand him at all. How can he? For certainly he has never been one to know the Lord's thoughts, or to discuss them with Him, or to move the hands of God by prayer. But, strange as it seems, we Christians actually do have within us a portion of the very thoughts and mind of Christ" (I Corinthians 4:9-16 *The Living Bible*).

Pardon me if I say "Hallelujah!!"

In the next chapter, Paul talks to them about the word entrusted to him and to Apollos, lovingly scolding them, it appears, for jealousy, division and quarreling. "There you are," he says, "quarreling about whether I am greater than Apollos, and dividing the church. . . . Who am I, and who is Apollos, that we should be the cause of a quarrel? Why, we're just God's servants, each of us with certain special abilities, and with our help you believed. My work was to plant the seed in your hearts, and Apollos' work was to water it, but it was God, not we, who made the garden grow in your hearts. The person who does the planting or watering isn't very important, but God is important because he is the one who makes things grow. Apollos and I are working as a team, with the same aim, though each of us will be rewarded for his own hard work. We are only God's co-workers. You are *God's* garden, not ours; you are *God's* building, not ours" (I Corinthians 3:4-9 *The Living Bible*).

Paul then draws the picture of a building—as he patiently shows them that brethren in Christ can differ in their belief and experience, and yet still be brothers, so long as they are each standing on *the one sure foundation, Jesus Christ Himself* (verses 10-11).

Take a look look at that picture. Read the chapter and see very clearly what a simple foundation this building has—Jesus. Jesus. Jesus.

As I look at Church history, it becomes *so* clear that the whole "church world"—Christianity at large has been split apart over the beliefs of men like Martin Luther, John Wesley, John Calvin and Alexander Campbell (to name just a few). In each case, *the division came when the "establishment felt compelled to withdraw"* from what they considered to be those "poor misguided individuals" who had the audacity to go their own way, believe their own understanding of the Bible, and *to choose God,* as they had come to know Him, *rather than the majority.*

One of the few words I remember from my three years of Greek (my college language) is *e/c/clesia*—the word which we translate *church.* It literally means "the called out." Christ's body is made up of "called out" people!

Called out of What?

Called out of the world, traditions of men, human thought systems; called out of "rational," practical life-styles, "safe" religion, dependence on social acceptance; *called out* of everything humanly limited—to a supernatural relationship with God, through His Son!

The Lord is building His church, person by person (Acts 2:42) like bricks in a wall—by calling each of us out from the familiar, the known, the natural—to the miraculous!

Don't you see that's the *only* way spiritual unity can be achieved—the kind of unity Paul describes as the ideal in I Corinthians twelve? *We must take our petty limits off God.* That means a recognition of the power of the Holy Spirit in the individual believer's life. That means *trusting* Him to shape and instruct each disciple! Listen to what Paul says: "Now God gives us many kinds of special abilities, but it is the same Holy Spirit who is the source of them all. There are different kinds of service to God but it is the same Lord we are serving. There are many ways in which God works in our lives, but it is the same God who does the work in and through all of us who are his. The Holy Spirit displays God's power through each of us as a means of helping the entire church" (I Corinthians 12:4-47 *The Living Bible*).

Paul speaks of the body as having many parts, "But the many parts make up only one body when they are all put together. So it is with the 'body' of Christ. Each of us is a part of the one body of Christ. Some of us are Jews, some are Gentiles, some are slaves and some are free. But the Holy Spirit has fitted us all together into one body. We have been baptized into Christ's body by the one Spirit, and have all been given that same Holy Spirit" (verses 12, 13 *The Living Bible*).

Paul proceeds to show that the Church is a living organism, exactly like the human body. He explains that while we have many "members," or many parts in our bodies, each one is necessary to the life and well-being of all. The loss of any one part of the body is *a mutilation of the body*.

What a glorious parallel this is—the body and the church! It's so very easy to understand. No statement of the unity that Jesus means to exist in the Christian Church could be more clear than what Paul is talking about right here. Nor could anything have come to the antagonistic, hate-and-fear-filled society of the Jews and Gentiles with more startling impact than this.

Imagine, mixing murderous Saul, the Jew, in the same body with proud Apollos the Gentile! Tax collectors and fishermen, prostitutes and royalty, Roman soldiers and Jewish priests! Only God, through miracles, could do it! And He did—and does.

If we could only see that body as God does,—as a gangly adolescent, with blemishes, bumps, squeaks and squawks, tripping over its too big feet, embarrassing itself constantly, alternately showing off and then wanting to hide, with Adam's apples and freckles and cowlicks and pigeon toes and knock-knees—but *growing, changing, maturing, being transformed by the heavenly hormonal power of the Holy Spirit* into the very likeness of Jesus!

11

THE BODY NEEDS A TUNE-UP!

That gangly, awkward, disjointed body called the church, is starting to come to life; to grow up!

I'm traveling all over the country these days, and often overseas, too. Everywhere, worldwide, there's a new stretching, scratching and self-examination going on—I believe it's Jesus, the head, calling His body together, for *action!*

At the same time, I'm deeply grieved to read and hear of nationwide groups shrinking from vital, booming organisms to shriveling, dry, bewildered organizations—while many of their individual members move on and out into a deeper walk with Jesus through His Spirit. It's a real paradox that as the shell dies, a lot of its individual parts are springing to life.

I don't doubt that many of these church groups are motivated by a desire to "defend the Gospel" and their idea of "sound doctrine," and that they stifle spiritual liberty in good conscience; I've been on that side of the fence—but their unyielding, inflexible, intolerant resistance to the earnest dedication and spirituality of many of its members is leading directly to deep wounds in Jesus' body—just when He's telling it to get ready for the last major evangelistic thrust and *the showdown with Satan.*

How this must grieve the Father-heart of God!

It's like a great track man, a miler, coming down

with ptomaine poisoning—the morning of the most important race of his career!

When Paul talked about the body as having many parts in I Corinthians twelve, he spotlighted the absurdity of one member, a foot or a hand, refusing to function, or acting as though it had a life of its own—just because it had a different functional use. *He emphasizes the necessity for the Baptist hand to realize its need for the Catholic knee*—and the Pentecostal tongue. This, Paul says in the fourth chapter of Ephesians, is the only way the body can really grow to its intended size and image and devastating power.

You don't cut your nose off because it has a pimple, do you? Or put out an eye that's perpetually at cross-purpose with the other? The navel doesn't seem very important *now*—but it sure *was* once upon a time, when it was the sole conveyor of life and health. Be thankful for it! Man, I want every part of my equipment, and I want it in peak condition. And I want it to know it's appreciated!

"Now here is what I am trying to say: (Paul states) All of you together are the one body of Christ and each one of you is a separate and necessary part of it. Here is a list of some of the parts he has placed in his church, which is his body:

Apostles,

Prophets—those who preach God's Word,

Teachers,

Those who do miracles,

Those who have the gift of healing,

Those who can help others,

Those who can get others to work together,

Those who speak in languages they have never learned. Is everyone an apostle? Of course not. Is everyone a preacher? No. Are we all teachers? Of course not. Does God give all of us the ability to speak in languages we've never learned? Can just anyone understand and translate what those are saying who have that gift of foreign speech? No, but try your best to have the most important of these gifts" (I Corinthians 12:27-31 *The Living Bible*).

Now, I've got to make a major point. *Paul's not talking to churches.* He's not addressing this teaching to the Catholic and Baptist and Pentecostal and Adventist *churches,* calling them each members of Christ's body. *Paul is talking to individuals!* Catholic and Baptist and Pentecostal and Adventist *individuals!*

JESUS IS NEVER going to get all those organizations together into one functioning body. He's not even trying to, because He adds only individuals to His precious body, *one at a time* (Acts 2:47). And every one of those individual parts has blemishes and blind spots —as well as special abilities which Jesus is molding together into a perfect man. Incredible isn't it?

How can such unity be achieved? Not by human wisdom, not in a million years. But Paul had some time to study this "body principle" in a Roman prison. And from that sober perspective, the Holy Spirit gave him a divine "anatomy lesson" and we find it in Ephesians four:

"I beg you—I, a prisoner here in jail for serving the Lord—to live and act in a way worthy of those who have been chosen for such wonderful blessings as these. Be humble and gentle. Be patient with each other, making allowance for each other's faults because of your love. *Try always to be led along together by the Holy Spirit,* and so be at peace with one another. [Italics author's]

"We are all parts of one body, we have the same Spirit, and we have all been called to the same glorious future. For us there is only one Lord, one faith, one baptism, and we all have the same God and Father who is over us all, in us all, and living through every part of us. However, Christ has given each of us special abilities—whatever he wants us to have out of his rich storehouses of gifts . . .

Why is it that he gives us these special abilities to do certain things best? It is that God's people will be equipped to do better work for him, building up the church, the body of Christ, to a position of strength and maturity; until finally we all believe alike about our salvation and about our Saviour, God's Son, and

50

all become full-grown in the Lord—yes, to the point of being filled full of Christ.

"Then we will no longer be like children, forever changing our minds about what we believe because someone has told us something different, or has cleverly lied to us and made the lie sound like the truth.

"Instead, we will lovingly follow the truth at all times—speaking truly, dealing truly, living truly—and so become more and more in every way like Christ who is the Head of his body, the church. Under his direction the whole body is fitted together perfectly, and each part in its own special way helps the other parts, so that the whole body is healthy and growing and full of love" (Ephesians 4:1-7, 11-16 *The Living Bible*).

12

THE GAMALIEL ATTITUDE

May I introduce you to Rabbi Gamaliel?

It may be that you've met before, in the pages of the New Testament—maybe not. In any case, I love this man for his common sense and for his kindly moderation. And, coming from a leading man in the Jewish Council, a doctor of the law, *a Pharisee by profession and religion,* his advice to the legalists of his day is amazing!

Rabbi Gamaliel was the teacher of Saul of Tarsus.

Yes, Saul had been brought up "at Gamaliel's feet." This is the same Saul who was obsessed with utterly destroying the Christians, breathing "threatenings and slaughter" against this Jesus "heresy"—until he was overpowered by the Holy Spirit. Gamaliel was a persuasive teacher and Saul, later to become Paul, was one of his star pupils.

Come with me to Acts five, where we see the apostles performing the extraordinary miracles which resulted in a rapid growth in the numbers of believers—and the Sadducees, filled with fear and envy, determining to stop it! As a result, the apostles are arrested and arraigned and the Council quickly decides to kill them (verse 33).

It is at this precise point that Gamaliel rises to the *defense* of the apostles—in my mind, he looks like a white-haired Perry Mason—and his deep-toned eloquence undoubtedly saves the lives of "our guys" at this time. Gamaliel's words to the Council are heavy with conviction as he counsels delay, inaction and caution. "Men of Israel," Gamaliel said, "take care what you are planning to do to these men!" (verse 35 *The Living Bible*). By way of example, he then reminds this highly-charged *"lynch mob"* about two popular uprisings which had utterly failed short years before. They had been left to fizzle out largely unopposed.

Stunned both by his position and his logic, the kill-crazy council hears Gamaliel sum up this way: "And so my advice is, leave these men alone. If what they teach and do is merely on their own, it will soon be overthrown. But if it is of God, you will not be able to stop them, lest you find yourselves *fighting even against God*" (verses 38, 39 *The Living Bible*).

Pretty good advice? I think so.

And the council did, too. They took Gamaliel's advice—at least, they didn't *kill* the apostles. They just beat them, ordered them to quit this talk of Jesus and miracles, and let them go.

How I wish this wise man was among us today! Many church councils could profit greatly from an hour or two with him. See, Gamaliel didn't have time—right in the middle of the repercussions of Pentecost—to adequately assess the claims and effects of Christianity in this new dimension; but he did give good advice under the circumstances. Wouldn't it be better *today* for us to study and watch what effects the current interest in the Holy Spirit may begin to have on Christians and the Church—to *judge the fruit* before we make any rash or rigid pronouncements?

If thousands, or millions, are led into a search for more of God in their personal lives, I believe He is able to lead us out of whatever error may creep into that new search. He did it in the 1st century! This will be especially true if these newly devoted, seeking Christians will plunge into the Word, pray more fervently, and ask God to take control of their lives— where they've been afraid or reluctant to do this in the past. And if the Holy Spirit is given freedom, this is the way He leads, gently but firmly.

I believe God can accomplish more with an earnest, enthusiastic seeker than a complacent, rather self-satisfied or apathetic member of some group.

What am I saying? I'm contrasting people who are awakened to the possibilities of God working in their lives in exciting dimension—to those who settle for a blind acceptance of a set of rules, self-denial, and occasional attendance at ritualistic services—all the while hoping somehow that God isn't watching what they're doing!

I'm just convinced God can lead and accomplish more with the first group than the second—and therefore we would do well to wait a little and see what God will do with "Church folks" who start to study and ask the Holy Spirit to be real to them. We might just really "come alive"; and if some human error is involved, as it most likely is in some instances, God can certainly help us to sort it out. Don't you think so? For too long the Church has been lukewarm—I think I'd rather have Him "sorting out" than "spewing out!"

Read again what Jesus said about the good wheat and the tares (Matthew 13:25-30).

Check me out, too, on this point: the only sins that furnish scriptural grounds for "disfellowshipping" are sexual and sensual sins, and teaching doctrines that deny the Sonship of Christ. Beyond, or apart from those things, it seems that the Bible allows for latitude of understanding and discernment among earnest men who confess Christ as Lord—not that God is happy with the latitude, but that He is *tolerant* and *merciful,* knowing full well our human faults and failings.

Remember what Jesus said about the mote and beam—"in your *brother's* eye?" (Matthew 7:3).

God, Who made us, knows that the Christians' adventures are a growth process, and that we'll all have "fallen short" and still be imperfect in our understanding when we *die*. But He has assured us in His Word that "the unity of the Spirit" must, and can, transcend all imperfections of our humanness and our intellectual divisions.

Lots of things have come up, in every age, to divide the Church of Jesus into camps. They always will, as long as the church is made of people. But our commission is to consciously *work for harmony* in the body. The divisions always occur between over-zealous advocates on the one hand and rigid defenders of opposite views on the other. Each is intolerant of the other.

The Apostle Paul fitted neither of these descriptions.

Though he'd been a "fire-breathing" legalist, Jesus made him the advocate of love (I Corinthians 13), and brotherhood, and tolerance and patience. Paul said, "He that is spiritual judgeth all things, yet *he himself is judged of no man*" (I Corinthians 2:15). That is quite a claim!

My wife, Shirley, and I have been accused of being over-zealous advocates, particularly because of experiences related in our previous books. But we have not tried to bind anybody else with our beliefs—we've simply felt led to share our views and our experiences, for whatever inspiration they may be to others. If divisions come (and I pray they won't) either as a result of our experiences or those of others, I'm afraid they'll be brought about by the Sauls among us—not the Pauls!

That's why I wanted us to visit with Gamaliel! He'd already seen enough, and heard enough, to know *something* was happening—and that it might be God! He and the other troubled religious leaders could see that Peter and James and John "had been with Jesus," through their love and the miracles that accompanied their ministry.

And now, miracles were about to happen to Gamaliel's star pupil, Saul of Tarsus! Boy, I wish I could have seen his reaction to that! Maybe our loving Lord used that miracle to draw the old teacher into the Spirit-filled life. I hope so.

What is the issue, really, at its core? It's a *yearning for deeper spirituality:* more earnest commitment; and joyful belief in the nearness and power of God *today* through His Spirit. If we're wrong or confused or over-zealous, please know that *God* will correct us—because we ask Him to. And He'll overrule in our influence on others too, for their sakes and the cause of the Gospel.

He can correct, chastise and redirect the earnest heart. But He has an awful time with the self-righteous one. Ask Paul.

13

TWENTIETH-CENTURY DIOTREPHES

In simple terms Paul said he preached "Christ, and Him crucified." *Isn't this the Gospel, and the Faith?* Isn't it faith in these fundamentals, and obedience to Christ's simple commands, that saves a person?

After that, there are many areas where the most brilliant among us disagree—but who is to say that *he* can decide the final answers to these weighty questions, and that all who disagree with him are damned?

If the individual Christian is not to work these things out with his Bible and God, if the majority opinion is to be the standard by which all individuals everywhere are to be judged faithful or unacceptable to God—then shouldn't we go ahead and write a Universal Creed, so that we can avoid the "chaos" and confusion that is inevitable when individuals are left to work out their own salvation? Wouldn't a fine scholarly set of rules, to which we all must agree be preferable to the unwritten creed we seem to have now?

As I look at it, this *unwritten* creed is an insidious thing; it varies from place to place, from preacher to preacher, from Christian to Christian, yes and even from Scholar to Scholar! You're never quite sure, when you're in different parts of the country, whether you're an "acceptable" Christian or not, according to this *unwritten* creed. Maybe at last we need a standard, so that the individual can be relieved of having to make decisions himself, so that he can be sure he's acceptable to the Universal Church, so that he knows the absolute and final limits to what he has a right to ask God for, and what God *will* and *won't* do *for* and *through* him.

Maybe the early Catholics were right all along—the Bible *is* a dangerous book for the layman! What chance does he have to understand it for himself, anyway? And if he finds himself out of step with the accepted scholarship and majority view, regardless of his spirituality or the experience he may have had with God himself, he is subject to excommunication—so he'd better leave the Book to the scholars and clergy. After all, if he starts reading and studying that Bible for himself, and in prayer and fasting and commitment of his life to his God, he will find himself doing his *own* thinking and having his *own* views and his *own* personal relationship with our Father. If his views and relationship clash in any significant detail with preachers who've been teaching it differently for thirty or forty years, he may find himself on the outside looking in! And who wants that? Better leave the imponderable Book alone, and let others do his thinking, and maybe even his praying, for him.

As I have pondered this, the thought has occurred that perhaps I should draft such a creed; however, I do not feel equal to that grave responsibility. Instead, may I set before you the following proposal:

What so many have sensed, but have been reluctant to propose, I now thrust before the concerned Christian brotherhood in the form of a motion: we need, and therefore nominate _____ as first Emperor of the Universal Church!

Though this idea may seem repugnant to a die-hard few, and even seem contrary to Biblical misunderstanding about the supposed "autonomy of the individual Christian and congregation," the church today is in chaos! A growing number of so-called "Christians" are presuming to read and interpret the Bible for *themselves!* And in many cases, some of these individuals are coming to conclusions, and even airing views *in public,* that clash with long-accepted, *unquestioned* dogmas of our brotherhood! This must be stopped, at all costs, even the cost of our individual freedom in Christ! This anarchy must cease!

There's only one way: *we must have an infallible authority to interpret the Scriptures for the masses,* and his authority must be absolute; otherwise, since there are several among us who feel they too are entitled to this authority, there will be endless wrangling among even the experts, and the masses will still be left in doubts and confusions, and want to "work out their own salvation." To utilize these other infallible men, whose judgments differ from the Emperor's, perhaps His Holiness will want to institute a College of Spiritual Knights where they can conduct their endless disputations out of sight of the brotherhood, and still with a great feeling of prominence.

I nominate _____ for the following reasons: though there are a number of other scholarly, dedicated and widely recognized authorities on every jot and tittle of the Law of Christ, there is none who has so demonstrated the fantastic ability to voraciously read and assimilate practically everything that his brethren everywhere read, state or think; to pounce immediately upon their every error, stated or implied, and rush it into print all over the country; and even though he admits he has "no divine inspiration," to infallibly ascertain even the hidden inner motives and twisted thought processes of his blundering, misguided flock and brilliantly project them into the future, constructing whole False Churches and Doomed Millions upon their exposed misconceptions! And although many among us find fault and mercilessly condemn others, there is none other with the Supreme self-confidence of _____ who can strike terror into the heart of the poor dumb ordinary Christian just by his piercing rhetoric and his soul-skinning, marrow-scorching pronouncements, which carry the finality of Eternal Doom!

Who else in our fellowship can perceive like the hawk, scent like the hound, ferret like the mole, pounce unsuspected like the mongoose, and quickly dispatch like the pirana? Who else can so ferociously and completely tear a brother, dedicated and honestly misguided though he be, to pieces before the whole Church—and yet claim to do so *in love and humility?*

59

I tell you, we must have this man as our unquestioned leader!

And the second proposal: in keeping with tradition which we have long ignored (to our harm) we should bestow upon this eminent brother a new name, befitting his position. There is only one possibility—*Diotrophes*. His High Holiness, Emperor Diotrephes of Third John who is the only man mentioned by name in the New Testament who had sufficient brilliance and infallible judgment to confidently reject the beloved Apostle John, and to *cast out of the church* those who opposed him! (III John, verse 9 and 10). Now brethren, we have some powerful and self important men in our church, no question—but we need one with the preeminence, the unshakable self-confidence, the unfailing energy and natural ability to stun and silence dissenters in our ranks; in short, a 20th Century Diotrephes. _____ is that man.

I recommend his election by acclamation, his modest protests notwithstanding. Though he may vocally deny his qualifications—his Pharisaical talent, and his actual quest for this position have long been demonstrated by his actions, his rigid positions on all issues, his stinging denouncements of all who dared disagree with him, and his quick readiness to disfellowship all "brethren" who couldn't come quickly to his personal understandings. He is a man of trigger-decision, instant action, and no sense of personal intellectual fallibility. He has exhausted the research possibilities on all matters necessary for salvation and acceptability to God, and has the final and unchangeable answers to all necessary questions. Why should he not be our final authority?

One note: I leave the blank spaces for the reader to fill in, with the name of your candidate. I have my own, of course, but I am just a mortal, and aware of it, and must confess that your man just may be as qualified as mine. But act now! Let the majority decide, for the last time, and let's be done with the confusion and worry of trying to figure things out for ourselves! While we have a man with these qualifications, at just the time when the Church needs his talents, let's vote him into office and beg him to instruct us!

Until we do, I must founder around, like most other seekers after righteousness, coming up with my *own* answers, based only on the Bible, God's answers to *my* prayers, and discussions with other individuals seeking after truth who also must shamefully confess to being just ordinary men and women.

How long must this go on? Till I die? Till eternity? Must I meet my Maker on my *own* merits, judged by my own decisions, my own study and service? Must I go on endlessly, not knowing whether I am finding favor with God and the brotherhood, like Paul in I Corinthians 4:1-5 and poor Apostle John?

Emperor Diotrephes forbid!

14

THE UNPARDONABLE SIN

It scares me to see so many people resisting the sovereign work of the Holy Spirit today. If I read my Bible correctly, according to Jesus' own words, there is one sin which cannot be forgiven—and that is speaking against the Holy Spirit (Matthew 12:31,2).

Jesus suffered many things without condemning during His earthly ministry; but *His harshest condemnation came upon those who attributed the work of the Holy Spirit to Satan*. This unforgivable offense is not somebody's faulty doctrinal concept—we're all imperfect there—but it is blasphemy against the Holy Spirit, and that's a most serious charge.

I know that what the Holy Spirit is doing shocks and violates the doctrinal concepts of many, but it is His doing nonetheless. The Holy Spirit has shocked *me* a lot of times, too! Jesus aggravated the religious authorities of His day when He simply would not revere the Sabbath habits and other traditions as strictly as they thought He ought to. But after all, He was and is the Son of God.

No man can instruct Him!

Paul says it bluntly: "For who hath known the mind of the Lord, that he may instruct Him?" (I Corinthians 2:16).

We see Jesus as the Agent of the Holy Spirit in particular, in Matthew's gospel, chapter twelve. Wherever

Christ went His hand was outstretched to heal and help. The convincing evidence of His miracles enraged the Pharisees and we see them holding a council meeting to plot Jesus' arrest and death. The thing that really vexed the Pharisees was the fact that not only by His miracles did He eclipse them, but the doctrine He preached was directly in opposition to their pride, hypocrisy, and worldly interest. They pretended, however, to be displeased at His breaking the sabbath day, which according to *their* law, was a capital crime.

Jesus knew what they were planning, and left the synagogue, with many following him (Matthew 12:15). His hour was not yet come, and He quietly withdrew from their presence into privacy and obscurity for the time. Still later in that chapter, Jesus can be observed once more in glorious conquest of Satan. "Then a demon-possessed man—he was both blind and unable to talk—was brought to Jesus, and Jesus healed him so that he could both speak and see. The crowd was amazed. "Maybe Jesus is the Messiah!" they exclaimed.

"But when the Pharisees heard about the miracle they said, 'He can cast out demons because he is Satan, king of devils.' " (verses 22-24 *The Living Bible*).

That miracles were being performed, Jesus' enemies could not deny. They were happening right before their eyes! Such superhuman power *must* have been divine or demonic—and the Pharisees accepted the latter choice. They were being driven nearly wild as the people's esteem of Jesus increased. Pride, superciliousness, and diabolical envy mercilessly goaded the Pharisees to vilify Jesus, speaking with disdain as they blasphemed against Him! Nothing could be more false and vile than this; that He, who is Truth itself, should be mentioned in combination with the father of lies, Beelzebub.

Among the fallen angels, the devils, there is a prince—the ringleader of the apostasy from God and the rebellion against him. He is the chief of the gang of infernal spirits, this Beelzebub—and for the Pharisees to accuse *Jesus* of a secret compact with Satan himself was equivalent to joining the demons' own rebellion against God!

Jesus knew the thoughts of His accusers, just as He knows the thoughts of all men. What they said was rooted in hate. And He knew it.

So, as He often did, He turned their own tradition against them.

There were those among the Jews who, as exorcists, claimed to be casting out demons and were approved by the Pharisees; in fact, the Jewish exorcists naturally gave the Spirit of God credit for what they were able to do. They could not condemn exorcism; and they *saw* Jesus scattering demons everywhere He went; so the only course left then was to charge that Satan was masterminding a fiendish plot through Jesus, allowing his own devils to be cast out!

As Jesus faced His accusers that day, His own sense of God's honor rose within Him, and the unshakeable truth that has stood the test of time was revealed. "He that is not with me is against me, and he that gathereth not with me scattereth abroad" (verse 30).

Look carefully, through 2000 years of history, at that statement.

Division will end in desolation; clashing must result in breaking; if we divide one from another, we become easy prey to our common enemy, none other than Satan himself.

And while thousands are being blessed as they come into the fullness of the Holy Spirit today, *horrible calamities* are coming upon those who are found resisting this great sweep of God. No one can maliciously ascribe the power of the Holy Spirit, and not be inducted into Satan's domain.

Jesus said it, not I.

"Even blasphemy against me or any other sin, can be forgiven—all except one: speaking against the Holy Spirit shall never be forgiven either in this world or in the world to come" (verses 31, 32 *The Living Bible*).

15

ADMONITIONS AND WARNING

Somebody said once that Judaism was "Christianity under a veil."

The more I study in the Old Testament, the more clearly I see how true that is!

The gospel—the good news about God's love, protection and power—was preached to the Jewish nation in their legal rites and sacrifices; and then, later, Christ Himself came and fulfilled Messianic prophecy.

When the Apostle Paul came on the scene, having been richly schooled in Old Testament Judaism, and having *met the Messiah* in person on the Damascus road, he looked back into all that familiar Jewish history—and suddenly the lights came on! He saw, as if for the first time, how incredibly patient God has been with the children of Israel, how mighty in His protection, how loving in His provision—and yet Paul could also feel God's angry pain when His children turned away and spurned His miraculous preparation for them.

Paul himself had resisted God—and had been struck blind! He knew from personal experience that even God's patience had limits, and he wrote his Hebrew Christian brothers in Corinth: "moreover, brethren, I would not that ye should be ignorant" (I Corinthians 10:1).

He warned them not to neglect the gifts and provision of God and the guidance of the Holy Spirit, not to begin to trust in human substitutes and religions, like their ancestors did before them: "God guided them by sending a cloud that moved along ahead of them; and he brought them all safely through the waters of the Red Sea. This might be called their 'baptism'—baptized both in sea and cloud! As followers of Moses—their commitment to him as their leader. And by a miracle, God sent them food to eat and water to drink there in the desert; they drank the water that Christ gave them. He was there with them as a mighty Rock of spiritual refreshment. Yet after all this, most of them did not obey God, and he destroyed them in the wilderness" (I Corinthians 10:1-5 *The Living Bible*).

It's hard to comprehend, to understand their waywardness, isn't it?

In spite of their unique position and the mercies, the miracles, that God bathed them in, the Israelites constantly looked for some substitute. This unchanging Father and His ten commandments didn't appeal to their human natures, and His miracles actually frightened them! Paul hoped the Corinthians would get the obvious connection—and I hope *we* do, too.

The particular climactic episode Paul was referring to can be found in Numbers thirteen and fourteen. You can look it up, and when you do, you'll catch the astounding sight of *two and a half million* children of Israel being turned away from the very borders of Canaan, right at the moment when they were ready to set foot in it—after those long torturous days of wandering in the wilderness!

Because of their murmuring and unbelief, there was a fatal quarrel between God and Israel. Even Moses' tearful intercession couldn't quench God's anger! The mutiny and rebellion of the people, their frightened refusal to accept His provision had brought God to the place where He determined to *destroy* them! But Moses, in one of the most dramatic moments in human history, persuaded the Creator to change His mind. Still, drastic judgment was coming.

It had taken them forty days to look over and reject His gift of the promised land, God proclaimed as He simmered to a slow boil, and now his stubborn children would *pay* for their faithlessness—a year of wandering for each day, bearing the burden of their sins. "I will teach you what it means to reject me," God said. "I, Jehovah, have spoken. Every one of you who has conspired against me shall die here in the wilderness" (Numbers 14:34, 35 *The Living Bible*).

Paul wrote this to the Corinthians. But have we forgotten that his letter has our names at the top of it, too (I Corinthians 1:2)?

Have we missed the parallel in our lives as Christians today?

One of the major similarities is that *we see ourselves and our God too small.*

In Numbers thirteen, the people lamented that as they looked at the enemies and the physical circumstances they felt they were as "grasshoppers" (verse 33). But in their paralyzing fear they also made the all-powerful, omnipotent God seem a "grasshopper" too. They distrusted God's strength on their behalf. They just disregarded the miracles and evidences of His presence that had led them all the way from Egypt.

And so God let them live, according to their own "self-vision," and die—as grasshoppers in the desert. Aren't we like the fearful, intimidated children of Israel?

We so often, in the wilderness of the 20th century, ignore and resist the obvious signs that God is giving us (Numbers 14:11) because they don't fit our "rational" concept. The obstinate and small-minded unbelief of the children of Israel actually caused God to break His promise to them (14:34)! "Ye shall know my breach of promise," God says.

It was the *children* of the disobedient Hebrews who finally walked into the promised land—by faith.

Twice Paul says, *"Now these things happened unto them for examples*—as object lessons to us—to warn us against doing the same things; they were written down so that we could read them and learn from them in these last days as the world nears its end. So be careful . . ." (I Corinthians 10:6, 11, 12a *The Living Bible*).

Nothing in scripture is written in vain. Its author, the Holy Spirit, is able to say exactly what He means. Therefore—we Christians are warned, with a monumental admonition, not to make the same mistake the Hebrew children made! We are to enter into the full miraculous provision of our Father, in the Kingdom of Christ—*now!* (Hebrews 3:7-12).

And isn't it wonderful that we can do that *individually?*

In Numbers fourteen God makes one exception in His condemnation of the Israelites. He says, "My servant Caleb is a different kind of man—he has obeyed me fully. I will bring him into the land he entered as a spy, and his descendants shall have their full share of it" (Verse 24 *The Living Bible*). Now get this: the King James translation says of Caleb *"he had another spirit with him!"* (verse 24). What do you suppose that means? Well, one obvious conclusion is that Caleb was drawing on a supernatural resource that gave him greater faith—and greater power!

This is like a lightning flash to me!

God is doing some mighty things today—because the time is short. He *is* pouring out His Spirit upon all flesh and His sons and daughters today *are* prophesying. They, too, have "another spirit" like Caleb did. Now, *we* can either hang back and deny that what is happening in our midst is of God and refuse to examine and really "go in and see"; or we can humbly and joyfully submit to being filled with His Spirit and being used as He chooses. We can go in and "possess the kingdom" and "occupy 'til He comes."

Which way seems right to you?

I can only echo what Paul said in his admonition and warning: "Wherefore let him that thinketh he standeth *take heed lest he fall*" (verse 12). "You are intelligent men," Paul continued, "judge what I say."

Dear Friend, the Spirit in Paul was speaking to *believers,* baptized, born-again children of God! Just like the Israelites who had come through the Red Sea, and

68

been blessed spiritually and materially through God's miraculous provision, we come now to a choice—to accept or reject the supernatural dimension of the baptism with the Holy Spirit!

You have a right to it; God has provided it for all who ask. You need it, for increased faith, love and power. (Romans 5:5, Acts 1:8 and 4:31, and I Corinthians 2:5 and 12:9).

And God wants you to be filled with His Spirit, for powerful kingdom living *now!* (Corinthians 4:20, Eph. 5:18 and 6:10-18).

So, here you stand, trembling on the bank of the River Jordan, looking over into the promised land, the kingdom in which God gives supernatural power and provision. You long to enter into a dimension of life in which the Lord brings triumph in every test—and yet, you hold back. I know the feeling: you *want* to be filled with God's Spirit, but you're afraid of the consequences, afraid of where God may lead you, afraid of what others will think, afraid of what it may cost you. I've been there.

Dear believing friend, listen again to your brother Paul: "Speak to each other about these things every day while there is still time, so that none of you will become hardened against God, being blinded by the glamor of sin. For if we are faithful to the end, trusting God just as we did when we first became Christians, we will share in all that belongs to Christ.

"But *now* is the time. Never forget the warning, '*Today* if you hear God's voice speaking to you, do not harden your hearts against him, as the people of Israel did when they rebelled against him in the desert.'

"And who were those people I speak of, who heard God's voice speaking to them but then rebelled against him? They were the ones who came out of Egypt with Moses their leader. And who was it who made God angry for all those forty years? These same people who sinned and as a result died in the wilderness. And to whom was God speaking when he swore with an oath that they could never go into the land he had promised

69

his people? *He was speaking to all those who disobeyed him*. And why couldn't they go in?

Because they didn't trust him." (Hebrews 3:13-19 *The Living Bible*).

16

THIS MATTER OF UNQUESTIONING FAITH

Don't quit now! Even if you've postponed your decision to enter in, go on and read the fourth chapter of Hebrews. After being exposed to the fearsome anger of God toward those of His kids who won't move on with Him, you really need a glimpse of mountain top living inside the kingdom, provided for those who *do* go in.

And, shining there like a magnificent, mysterious diamond—is the key to the kingdom!

Paul says: "Although God's promise still stands—his promise that all may enter his place of rest—we ought to tremble with fear because some of you may be on the verge of failing to get there after all. For this wonderful news—the message that God wants to save us—has been given to us just as it was to those who lived in the time of Moses. But it didn't do them any good because they didn't believe it. *They didn't mix it with faith.* For only we who *believe* God can enter into his place of rest. He has said, 'I have sworn in my anger that those who don't believe me will never get in,' even though he has been ready and waiting for them since the world began" (Hebrew 4:1-3 *The Living Bible*).

The key to the kingdom is faith.

Since man's beginning in Eden, the Lord God has demanded almost blind, unquestioning faith of His creatures. And He rewards it! But to test our faith, He often requires "irrational" things, including the total surrender of our wills to His.

For some time I sought an experience in the Holy Spirit that I hoped would *create* faith. But that experience didn't come. It was only when I utterly surrendered my will to Christ, not counting the cost (in terms of personal pride or whatever), and stepped out on what the Bible calls "the very substance of things hoped for" that the experience came—and I began to realize what *unquestioning believing faith* really was.

We so seldom mix our faith with what we hear; like Paul says, we listen not, and go about our business. The word, no matter how well it's preached, will not get the job done by itself!

'Through all the long ages there have been many "unprofitable hearers"—many who hear sermons, but whose souls do not profit thereby. Why? Because—*What we hear must be mixed with faith.* Faith must mingle with every word we hear and read for ourselves. And as James says, "faith without works (corresponding *action)* is dead!" After we have read and/or heard the word, then we must assent to the truth of it, approve it, accept the provision it offers, *act* on it (apply the word to ourselves with whatever emotional response the Spirit moves within our deepest inner recesses)—and then we profit immeasurably by the word preached.

There is no better definition of *faith* than Paul's in Hebrews eleven. "What is faith? It is the confident assurance that something we want *is going to happen.* It is the *certainty* that what we hope for is waiting for us, even though we cannot see it up ahead. Men of God in days of old were famous for their faith."

Dear friend, please read the entire eleventh chapter of Hebrews. Let your mind be assaulted with the staggering, incredibly "irrational" things God has required of so many of His servants. He didn't expect what He was requiring of them *to make sense.* He simply expected unquestioning faith. Their faith was a faith of consent; of child-like submission. Faith, to be real like that, will first move upon our affections, then our actions. Does that sound backwards? Well, Paul says it clearly in Romans 10:10, "with the *heart* man believes unto righteousness"!

Faith will finally silence objections.

Noah didn't dispute with God about why he should build an ark. He might well have, "rationally"; he was building the thing one hundred twenty years and, after all, there was no sign whatsoever of a flood!

"Noah's belief in God was in direct contrast to the sin and disbelief of the rest of the world—which refused to obey—and because of his faith he became one of those whom God has accepted" (verse 7 *The Living Bible*).

Now, if you really want your mind "blown"—short circuited—put yourself in Abraham's place! Imagine being told to take your son, *your only son,* and offer him up as a burnt offering. You're over one hundred twenty years old and your grown son, Isaac is the one God promised and gave you miraculously! You love him more than your own life. Could you—would you—do such a crazy, irresponsible thing?

Abraham did.

I really believe that God so loved Abraham, trusted him enough, that He could share with him some of the pain He would feel when His own son would be offered up as a sacrifice on Calvary—and there would be no one to take His place. And old Abraham loved God so much that he was willing to share that burden, though he'd never heard of a cross. Abraham could show that kind of faith because "he trusted in God and His promises" (verse 17). And Paul says elsewhere, that God declared the old man righteous—because he *believed* (Galatians 3: 6, 7).

The writer calls these heroes of the faith "a great cloud of witnesses" (Hebrews 12:1)—and I suspect they're watching us now, rooting for us to believe and act, like they did.

I'm sure they sympathize deeply with us when we go

through some dark test or trial; and I expect they chuckle some when they see us have to suspend reason to act by faith—to do some impractical, unnatural, humanly senseless thing, just to obey the Lord. After all, *they* each had to!

Paul says flatly that *"without faith it is impossible to please him:* for he that cometh to God must believe that he is, and that he is a rewarder of them that diligently seek him"* (Verse 6). My wife and I have experienced the reality of this. We *did* continually seek God and we *did* expect Him to reward our diligent search—and praise the living God, He *did* just that! Hallelujah!

I don't expect everyone, not even my believing Christian brothers, to fully understand the miracles God performed as He answered our prayers; but I simply must say joyfully and gratefully that He *has,* and *continues* to!

After the long list of ancient heroes in the "roll call of faith" chapter (Hebrews II)—which if you know the Lord, should have you tingling to your toes—Paul brings them and us to our knees before the greatest Believer of all eternity, Jesus the Son of God.

"Look to Jesus," Paul cries in Hebrews 12:2 "the author and finisher of our faith"! Faith is a supernatural gift that originates—and ends in Him alone.

Talk about faith! Jesus believed, not just in God and His provision, but in you! He staked His life on your willingness to believe Him and follow His example. And He works with those who do—personally! (Mark 16:20).

You can almost hear the shouts of the "cloud of witnesses" cheering us on, telling us *there is unbelievable power in faith* (Hebrews 12).

Every one of those witnesses was called on to do something foolish—just because God said so. Every one *had to die to his own intellect* and reason. Every one of these took the chance that others would despise and ridicule, and reject him—and he obeyed God anyway. And every one is in paradise now, continuing to taste the rich provision of God for those who take His word literally—and mix it with faith!

74

Which brings us back to our starting point, the 4th chapter of Hebrews. I promised we'd see the mighty, mysterious key to the kingdom—and we have. It's faith.

And I promised we'd glimpse some mountain top living, in the kingdom—and we have. *And we can get in on it;* that's the best part!

"But Jesus the Son of God is our great High Priest who has gone to heaven itself to help us; therefore let us never stop trusting Him. This High Priest of ours understands our weaknesses, since He had the same temptations we do, though he never once gave way to them and sinned. So let us come boldly to the very throne of God and stay there to receive his mercy and to find grace to help us in our times of need. (Hebrews 4:14-16 *The Living Bible*).

And the only way to get there is to use the KEY.

17.

THE BASIS FOR BROTHERHOOD

"Now I beseech you, brethren, by the name of our Lord Jesus, that ye all speak the same thing, and that there be no divisions among you; but that ye be perfectly joined together in the same mind and in the same judgment. For it hath been declared unto me of you, my brethren, by them which are of the house of Chloe, that there are contentions among you. Now this I say, that every one of you saith, I am of Paul; and I of Apollos; and I of Cephas; and I of Christ. Is Christ divided? Was Paul crucified for you, or were ye baptized in the name of Paul?" (I Corinthians 1:10-13) "For ye are yet carnal: for whereas there is among you envying and strife, and divisions, are ye not carnal, and walk as men? For while one saith, I am of Paul; and another, I am of Apollos; are ye not carnal?" (I Corinthians 3:3 and 4).

Was the Holy Spirit powerless to bring about unity in the First Century? Or was He hampered, even with the gifts of the Spirit operating, by human weakness, finite understanding, tricks and wiles and counterfeiting of the Devil, and man's egocentric desire to "lord it over" others?

A quick review of 1st and 2nd Corinthians and Galatians will give you the answer. The baptism of the Holy Spirit didn't make men suddenly perfect—in deed or doctrine!

As He was restricted in the First Century only by man's failure to yield to Him—so I believe the Holy Spirit is restricted today. But God Himself chose to put this treasure—His own Holy Breath—in "earthen vessels" (II Corinthians 4:7).

So, any discussion of the work of the Holy Spirit must be approached in a spirit of humility and love and brotherhood—and never from a position of condemnation or judgment. After all, only God can make any of us see His way of opening our individual understandings. It's a supernatural operation! Jesus Himself, on the road to Emmaus after His resurrection, rebuked His own disciples' "slowness of heart to believe" (Luke 24:25). And then He opened their eyes!

I pray He'll perform that spiritual surgery on us today.

It's only as we focus on Jesus—in the Word, in us, and in each other, and not on all the doctrinal differences that may exist—that He can bring us together. When we do this, and cease to judge each other as Paul clearly indicates *we must* in I Corinthians three and four, then we'll have taken a giant step toward unity of the Spirit. We can't achieve this unity by rational or human means. We can't shout other people down or even convince them by arguing theology or doctrinal points, in most cases. But individually yielding to the Spirit of God we will make it possible for Him to draw us together.

I believe this is the only way in which the unity of the Spirit will *ever* be achieved. Time is very short and I find myself praying more and more that God will draw His believing children together in spite of their differences—in the little time that remains before He comes.

The beloved apostle John, in I John gives us the basis for brotherhood—*belief in Jesus and confession that He is Lord.* We start from there, and grow at different rates toward maturity in Christ.

If we could only relax and let the Lord deal with us individually, how simple life in Jesus would be! He can and will work out our imperfections—but our efforts to

77

correct each other breed pride and resentments. Isn't that the black side of the history of religion?

Hatred is a sign of spiritual darkness. "Anyone who says he is walking in the light of Christ but dislikes his fellow man, is still in darkness. But whoever loves his fellow man is 'walking in the light' and can see his way without stumbling around in darkness and sin. For he who dislikes his brother is wandering in spiritual darkness and doesn't know where he is going, for the darkness has made him blind so that he cannot see the way" (I John 2:9-11 *The Living Bible*).

Jesus calls us to love—a forgiveness-from-the-cross kind of love. A "neither do I condemn thee" kind of love. It's this very kind of love—this, "You're my brother, in spite of our differences" kind of love—that identifies Jesus' people, that separates the sheep from the goats.

For one sure mark of those who belong to the devil, is *hatred of the brethren* (I John 3:12). "So now we can tell who is a child of God and who belongs to Satan. Whoever is living a life of sin and doesn't love his brother shows that he is not in God's family; for the message to us from the beginning has been that we should love one another. If we love other Christians, it proves that we have been delivered from hell and given eternal life. But, a person who doesn't have love for others, is headed for eternal death. *Anyone who hates his Christian brother is really a murderer at heart;* and you know that no one wanting to murder has eternal life within. We know what real love is from Christ's example in dying for us. And so we also ought to lay down our lives for our Christian brothers" (I John 3:10, 11, 14-16 *The Living Bible*).

So many of us have been willing to shed blood, alright. Our brother's!

Have we come very far since Cain and Abel? Remember—*their* fatal argument was over worship and sacrifice and who was more pleasing to God. We're still just outside the Garden. And the way back in is—obedience. It was *dis*obedience that got us kicked out, and only obedience to the Good Shepherd will lead us back, individually, to the Tree of Life. That Cain and Abel stuff—judging our brothers—will forever be outside the Garden.

Listen: "This is what God says we must do: Believe on the name of his Son Jesus Christ, and love one another. Those who do what God says—they are living with God and he with them. We know this is true because *the Holy Spirit he has given us* tells us so" (I John 3:23, 24 *The Living Bible*).

And listen again: *Hereby know we that we dwell in him, and He in us, because He hath given us of his spirit"* (I John 4:13, *KJV*).

18

GOD RESERVES THE RIGHT TO DEAL
WITH HUMAN BEINGS AS HE CHOOSES

Have you ever noticed how tough it was for Jesus to
communicate with the very ones He came to save?

It was murder—literally.

He was dealing with them face to face, God in
human flesh, and yet, over and over they seemed to
look at Him blankly, and completely miss the point of
what He was saying, even when He put it in the sim-
plest possible terms. His own disciples, even the twelve,
misunderstood Him often, and never fully grasped His
meanings until He was gone and the Holy Spirit began
to open their understanding and bring to their remem-
brance many of the things Jesus had said.

In Matthew sixteen, in less than ten verses, there's an
amazing, heartbreaking, frightening example.

Jesus said to Peter (when Peter answered Jesus'
question as to who He really was, and Peter replied,
"The Christ, the Messiah, the Son of the living God,"
(verse 15): "God has blessed you, Simon . . . for my
Father in heaven has personally revealed this to you—
when Jesus began to speak plainly to his disciples
about going to Jerusalem and what would happen to
him there—that he would suffer at the hands of the religious leaders, that he would be killed and that three
days later he would be raised to life again. . . . Peter
begged Him not to go (verses 21,22). Jesus turned on

Peter and said, "Get thee behind me, Satan . . . You are a dangerous trap to me! You are thinking merely from a human point of view, and not from God's" (verse 23).

Poor Peter. Can you identify with him?

Same apostle; same Christ; same mind and experience; but absolutely opposite results in his discernment of God's will and leading—all of this within the context of one brief encounter and conversation with our Lord.

We're all this way, no better nor worse than Peter; we're humans, trying to understand God's will. Even though we have it revealed and written down, we're still trying to understand perfection with imperfection —and with imperfect instruments.

It's tough.

The Apostle Paul talked about this; he calls it "seeing through a glass darkly." We understand "in part and we prophesy in part."

Even with the most brilliant human minds and understanding and scholarship, we're no better than Peter or Paul. Are we? The blame for our inability to communicate as fully as we'd like must be placed on our own finiteness. If Christ Himself failed to make His thinking and experiences clearly understood to those who heard Him speak—because of *their* human qualities, not His—and with the stupendous display of miracles, and the actual voice of God in the bargain—you and I shouldn't chide ourselves because we fail to understand each other one hundred percent!

Want to know another surprising thing?

Paul wasn't always sure, when he was speaking, whether it was his own understanding, or by inspiration of God's Spirit! In I Corinthians seven, he *says* that right out! There we hear him saying three or four times that he *thinks* he is giving counsel from God's Spirit (verses 6, 12, 25 and 40).

He wrote other letters to churches and individuals, as did the other apostles; I'm sure he and they gave those letters just as much thought and prayer, but God hasn't preserved them for us today. Either they weren't as fully inspired, or they weren't necessary for us. None of these writers knew which letters of God's Spirit would be preserved for the later church and which would be lost; it didn't matter. They were so yielded to God's will, that they did just what they felt led to do at the time, and left the working of God's infinite plan to Him. The lesson is clear: *God reserves the right to deal with human beings as He chooses.*

And am I glad He does! Because, obviously, most of the time we just don't know very much about His total operation or how Satan has bound and deceived others.

Can you appreciate Paul's admonition, "Stop evaluating Christians . . . by what they seem to be like on the outside" (II Corinthians 5:16 *The Living Bible*)?

As the time draws to a close and we approach the end of the age, we may all be doing a little rethinking about what the "gospel" is. I don't mean that we'll change our minds about Christ and salvation—that *is* the gospel! But beyond that, we may have to save some of our Special "add-on" doctrinal goodies 'til later. Our concerns about what a person does after he's "new-born" spiritually are important, but God's busy in the maternity ward right now—and there's no time to haggle over pet procedures!

We know what we believe, and we practice and teach it.

But Peter and the other apostles found out in the early days of the Church that God will constantly surprise us in His dealing with people—not for shock value, but because He knows us as individuals and because He is not static or legalistic or bound necessarily by our concepts. He is Creator—and Father—and Saviour; and the Designer of our fingerprints—no two alike! Yet, though we start out differently, we somehow wind up transformed into His image—by "you know who" (II Corinthians 3:17, 18)!!

Throughout the gospels—the record of Jesus' earthly life and ministry—there is mind-blowing evidence that God deals with people in a variety of ways. Just look at Mary Magdalene, Zaccheus, Matthew the publican, and the thief on the cross for a sampling! And Jesus made some very startling statements which at times, I'm sure, ran contrary to what His disciples expected Him to say. In John five, for instance, He states emphatically that "anyone who listens to my message and believes in God who sent me has eternal life, and will never be damned for his sins, but has already passed out of death into life" (verse 24).

We, as Christians, have a blessed privilege—it is showing others *by a demonstration in our own lives* that Jesus can take us from where we are—and lead us into greater and greater happiness and blessing and finally life eternal with God through His Son. That's the most effective sermon you can ever preach: your own changed life!

So, when someone tells me that He's a Christian, and he loves Jesus and has obeyed Him and shows some evidence of Christ in his life, I think I must give him the benefit of the doubt—even though I may find myself differing with him on doctrinal points. If I'm given the opportunity (as Aquilla and Priscilla were in the history of the early Church as related in the book of Acts) to instruct him and help him to gain some additional insight and understanding, some new enlightenment, then I thank God for the opportunity and do my best, being led by the Holy Spirit.

It's best to water after the seed has been planted; up 'til then, it doesn't do much good.

19

THE HOLY SPIRIT IS A PERSON, NOT A PRINTED PAGE

How would you like to be thought of as an "it"?

Well, that happens to the Holy Spirit all the time; millions of Christians including preachers and some theologians, refer to the Spirit of God as a "force," an "influence" even a "fluid"! Well, I've got great good news.

He is the third *Person* of the Godhead—He is a "Who."

From Genesis 1:20 to John 14:16 to Revelations 22:17, He is revealed as a Person, with power and intellect and emotion—not just information on a printed page with scattered references to "its" influence throughout the Bible. The glorious reality of *who* He is and *what* He does in the lives of believers has not broken through to most of us. There is even great fear on the part of many that if we admit to the powerful working of Holy Spirit in our lives, we may be labeling ourselves "freaks," "fanatics," or "Holy Rollers."

And, come to think of it, I guess some of that fear is well founded. Wherever the Spirit of God is given access to people's lives, He seldom preserves the status quo—He generally *changes* things!

He was never static, complacent or literary—just ask Moses. Ask David and Daniel and Joel. Ask Peter and

James and Jesus and Titus about the Holy Spirit's dynamic action in believers' lives.

Paul, speaking in defense of the outpouring of the Holy Spirit in his own experience, actually "brags" some about the changes in himself and the results of the Power of God working in him: "So it is right for me to be a little proud of all Christ Jesus has done through me. I dare not judge how effectively he has used others, but I know this: he has used me to win the Gentiles to God. I have won them by my message and by the good way I have lived before them, and by the miracles done through me as signs from God—*all by the Holy Spirit's power*" (Romans 15:17, 18 *The Living Bible,* itals. author's).

One of the common and natural tendencies among church people today is to discredit those whose experience with Jesus has been different from theirs.

My wife and I and our four girls are more wholeheartedly in love with Jesus and are more completely integrated into His body than ever before in our lives. But lots of folks find it very difficult to accurately evaluate our experiences—since they have no personal point of reference. They have their own cherished *doctrinal* views, but dissimilar experience!

"And because of what Christ did, all you others too, who heard the Good News about how to be saved, and trusted Christ, were marked as belonging to Christ by the Holy Spirit, who long ago had been promised to all of us Christians" (Ephesians 1:13).

Even the Apostle Paul saw the danger in assessing others by his own experience: "I dare not judge how effectively he (the Holy Spirit) has used others. . . ."

Lots of folks today are not as "timid" as Brother Paul, though!

There are just plenty of Christian people who feel fully qualified to "grade" other believers, almost like the man at the stockyards with the Government stamp in his hand. He inspects the meat and stamps some of it "U.S. Grade A Choice"—and lots of almost identical produce "unfit by Government standards."

That's fine when and where meat is concerned; but

where Christians are concerned, God Almighty wields the stamp—and the seal!

Let me illustrate the danger I see here.

Many times Christians "withdraw" from each other over doctrinal differences. Here's an example in II Thessalonians 3:6 and 14. "Now we command you, brethren, in the name of our Lord Jesus Christ, that ye withdraw yourselves from every brother that walketh disorderly, and not after the tradition *which he received of us.* . . . And if any man obey not our word *by his epistle,* note that man, and have no company with him, that he may be ashamed."

Usually, the "withdrawing" group uses the word *tradition* to refer to its own peculiar doctrinal belief. But wait!

The same Paul who wrote *that,* also wrote I Thessalonians 4:8; 5:19-20. In that *same epistle* we read: "He therefore that despiseth, despiseth not man, but God, who hath also given unto us His Holy Spirit. Quench not the Spirit. Despise not prophesyings."

And the *same* John who in II John 9-11 commanded "Whosoever transgresseth, and abideth not in the doctrine of Christ, hath not God. He that abideth in the doctrine of Christ, he hath both the Father and the Son. If there come any unto you, and bring not *this doctrine,* receive him not into your house, neither bid him Godspeed: For he that biddeth him Godspeed is partaker of his evil deeds." Here is a *doctrinal teaching* of John that reads: "And this is His commandment, That we should believe on the name of His Son Jesus Christ, and love one another, as He gave us commandment. And he that keepeth His commandments dwelleth in him, and he in him. And hereby we know that He abideth in us, by the Spirit which He hath given us. . . . *Hereby know we* that we dwell in Him, and He in us, *because He hath given us of His Spirit.* Whosoever shall confess that Jesus is the Son of God, God dwelleth in him, and he in God. . . . And there are three that bear witness in earth, the Spirit, and the water, and the blood: and these three agree in one."

Of course, John himself was "received not" "was

withdrawn from"—by Diotrephes, as recorded in III John 9 and 10.

There will always be the descendants of Diotrephes within church ranks whose roaring righteousness and vigilante complexes will imperil the growth and harmony of the Church. I can now begin to identify with the Apostle John. What he said makes sense to me now in a dimension and glory that I never understood before. "We know this is true (the fact that we can have clear consciences, coming to the Lord with perfect assurance and trust) because the Holy Spirit He has given us tells us so" (I John 3:24 *The Living Bible*).

But how can a person be expected to understand this if they haven't experienced it? *The Holy Spirit is more than an idea* or an attempt to make words spring to life in human action. He is a Person, and His Presence and direction in your life can be *felt*. Yes, the beloved Apostle John had experienced His presence, and so do we.

I love the way Paul teaches about this Third Person and his ministry through us: "Let love be your greatest aim; nevertheless, *ask also for the special abilities* the Holy Spirit gives, and especially the gift of prophecy, being able to preach the message of God. . . ." (I Corinthians 14:1, 36-39). Then later, as if sensing that some Diotrephes types would disagree with what he has been telling them, Paul adds, "You disagree? And do you think that the knowledge of God's will begins and ends with you Corinthians? Well, you are mistaken! You who claim to have the gift of prophecy or any other special ability from the Holy Spirit should be the first to realize that what I am saying is a commandment from the Lord Himself. But, if anyone still disagrees—well, we will leave him in his ignorance. So, my fellow believers, long to be prophets so that you can preach God's message plainly; and *never say it is wrong to 'speak in tongues';* however, be sure that everything is done properly in a good and orderly way."

By the time our brother Paul wrote this, he'd been taught beautifully by the Spirit to balance liberty with love, doctrine with divine independence. It hadn't been an easy education for a former fire-breathing pharisee!

Paul's exhortation to Titus directed him to be aware of the arch legalists of the day—those who claimed to have an air-tight patent on the truth. These were "Christian Pharisees" who evidently were assuming the spiritual leadership of the congregation of believers—and they could so easily lead the new Christians astray. This letter was written to Paul's young friend Titus in the church at Crete, where harsh legalism had combined with fleshly immorality to form an unruly, unspiritual body of believers. It's been said that "It is to the glory of Christianity that, in soil so unpromising, it produced the flower and fruit of faith and holiness."

But that same doctrinal letter contained these words: "When the time came for the kindness and love of God our Savior to appear, then He saved us—not because we were good enough to be saved, but because of His kindness and pity—by washing away our sins *and giving us the new joy of the indwelling Holy Spirit whom He poured out upon us with wonderful fullness*—and all because of what Jesus Christ our Savior did so that He could declare us good in God's eyes—all because of His great kindness; and now we can share in the wealth of the eternal life He gives us, and we are eagerly looking forward to receiving it" (Titus 3:4-7 *The Living Bible*).

There was one Power in creation greater than all the immoral legalism of some church "leaders"—the indwelling Holy Spirit! Praise Jesus!

And then there is another letter, sometimes called a fugitive letter, written by the Apostle Paul to an obscure group of Christians in the first century. This letter was destined to become the Magna Charta of spiritual freedom for the whole world and subsequently for all time. It's called the Epistle to the Galatians.

This letter contributed greatly to dispelling the spiritual darkness of the Middle Ages. As it has been said: "wherever religion has lost its reality, wherever ritual is more regarded than right living, *wherever subscription to creed is substituted for submission to Christ*, wherever loud claims of orthodoxy are accompanied by conduct devoid of charity, wherever deeds of selfright-eousness are obscuring the glory of the cross, there this epistle should be made to sound out its clarion call to a new dependence upon justifying grace, to a faith that is shown by works, to a walk that is by the Spirit, to a life inspired by love."

The Epistle to the Galatians was written by Paul to defend the purity of the gospel against those who were insisting that Christians must observe the Mosaic law. As you read it, you sense the personality and the painful experience of the great apostle clearly stamped in every utterance. There is a powerful mind, a tender heart, and an indomitable will—all tied together with the deepest spiritual insight. He had been the arch-legalist, the self-righteous vigilante, the "defender of truth"—and then he'd become the target of the same sort of men. He knew both sides of the game called "Righteousness Roulette"—now you're in, now you're out.

Catch the pathos then in what Paul says in Galatians 3:1-5: "Oh, foolish Galatians! What magician has hypnotized you and cast an evil spell upon you? For you used to see the meaning of Jesus Christ's death as clearly as though I had waved a placard before you with a picture on it of Christ dying on the cross. Let me ask you this one question: Did you receive the Holy Spirit by trying to keep the Jewish laws? Of course not, for *the Holy Spirit came upon you* only after you heard about Christ and trusted him to save you. Then have you gone completely crazy? For if trying to obey the Jewish laws never gave you spiritual life in the first place, why do you think that trying to obey them now will make you stronger Christians? You have suffered so much for the Gospel. Now are you going to just throw it all overboard? I can hardly believe it!"

"I ask you again, *does God give you the power of the Holy Spirit and work miracles among you* as a re-sult of your trying to obey the Jewish laws? No, of course not. It is when you believe in Christ and fully trust him."

His tone is severe, but the defection of these Galatian Christians was senseless and inexcusable. By some devious and subtle reasoning, the Judaizing teachers had beguiled the Galatians and Paul finds it necessary to rebuke them severely.

These Galatian Christians, like all other members of the First Century Church, had been granted miraculous spiritual gifts—such as prophecy, the gift of tongues, the interpretation of tongues, the gift of healing—these were the signs and seals of the new life which God in Christ, through the working of the Holy Spirit, had given them. They had been tremendously blessed and it had come about as a result of their *faith*—not through observance of ceremonial law, but through belief in Christ as a miracle-working Lord. Divine energy had been at work in their midst; they had been on a glorious pathway to advancement in things spiritual; but now they were actually starting a nose-dive from the plane of the Spirit to the level of the flesh, turning from that which was divine to that which was human. How deeply this hurt Paul! What folly he saw in their actions. He actually saw them walking in his footsteps —in *reverse!* They were starting to trade their spiritual liberty for Pharisaical bondage, whipped on and herded by self-appointed shepherds.

Paul goes on reminding them of Abraham's faith, showing them that "those who depend on the Jewish laws to save them are under God's curse, for the Scriptures point out very clearly, 'Cursed is everyone who at any time breaks a single one of these laws that are written in God's Book of the Law.' Consequently it is clear that no one can ever win God's favor by trying to keep the Jewish laws, because God has said that the only way we can be right in His sight is by faith. . . . But Christ has brought us out from under the doom of the impossible system by taking the curse for our wrongdoings upon Himself. . . . Now God can bless the Gentiles, too, with this same blessing he promised to Abraham; *and all of us as Christians can have the promised Holy Spirit through this faith*" (vss. 10, 11a, 13a, 14; itals. author's).

What's my point in all of this?

Dear friend, I simply hope to point you toward the Comforter, the Holy Spirit of God—and to help you see Him as a person who waits for your invitation to come dwell in your house and in your heart. He speaks to you from the pages of the Bible, true; but He is *not* that book—He is its Author!

Peter, by the Spirit's own urging, offers Him to every believer in Acts 2:38-39—'And Peter replied,' "Each one of you must turn from sin, return to God, and be baptized in the name of Jesus Christ for the forgiveness of your sins; then you also shall receive this gift, the Holy Spirit, *For Christ promised him to each one of you* who has been called by the Lord our God, and to your children and even to those in distant lands!"

Speak to this One, this promised Gift—right now—and tell Him He can have charge of your life, your intellect, your will, your heart. Invite Him in!

And then get ready for some wonderful changes!

that has worked. Our Lord is then reaching deep into
. . . unhindered action. (She wasn't even in the room
. . . . . Holy Spirit she have received until.)

20

A GIFT, BUT IT MUST BE RECEIVED

When I was growing up in Nashville, and spending a
lot of time in church, I had a real reluctance to talk
about Jesus to my friends or to anybody else.

As I look back now, I realize it was because *very little
had happened to me!*

I was *doing* many of the "right" things—I was at-
tending church services without fail, and I could mouth
a lot of the "right" things. But this, of course, is not the
basis for a vital relationshp with Jesus. Jesus gives the
basis for that relationship in John five: "You search the
Scriptures, for you believe they give you eternal life.
And the Scriptures point to me! Yet you won't come to
me so that *I can give you this life* eternal!"

I now see the necessity to come intimately and pri-
vately and wholly to *Jesus*—not just to the prescribed
doctrine of some church. Of course Jesus is the best
source and the surest foundation of all our doctrine;
and a meager bit of research on your own will turn up
many startling promises from His lips about the presence and the powerful working of the Holy Spirit in the
lives of believers.

Actually the fourth and fifth chapters of John are
incredibly rich in practical teaching. I wish all young
people would spend a month reading and thinking
through just those two chapters. They'd probably become dynamic, spirit-filled disciples a lot faster than

most church schools could produce them! In the fourth chapter, is the story of Jesus' encounter with the Samaritan Woman. Our Lord is seen revealing deep truth to an adulterous woman (she wasn't even a luke-warm "church-goer"; how could she have received truth?) and promising that every believer is entitled to a well of spiritual water, springing up inside him and gushing up into eternal life! (Doesn't that smack of "emotionalism"?)

And you know what? He's still meeting people like that and making the same offer!

Once the experience that Jesus described to Nicodemus in John three has occurred, the well begins to gush out and there's no stopping it! Jesus said, "What I am telling you so earnestly is this: Unless one is born of water and the Spirit, he cannot enter the Kingdom of God. Men can only reproduce human life, but *the Holy Spirit gives new life from heaven;* so don't be surprised at my statement that you must be born again!" (verses 5-7).

Doctrinal teaching alone, without an accompanying emphasis and teaching on the work of the Holy Spirit, suppresses and squelches the birth process Jesus was talking about. In doing this, the church today must face the fact that it is in danger of turning out spiritual mutants in young people, Christians whose bodies and minds mature, but whose spirits remain helpless and ignorant.

May I give you an example?

Our German shepherd, Heidi, gave birth to her first litter of pups a while back! It was her first time out, and though God built in certain instincts and intelligence, it became obvious that she needed a little outside help; some instruction. Because, when we looked out on the patio one morning, we saw a still, lifeless package that she had given birth to—and then left!

We ran out and Shirley saw immediately what the problem was: the pup was still in its little delivery sack —Heidi hadn't known to remove it! Shirley quickly tore it open, and this glorious little creature began to stir and writhe and ask for contact with its mama. It already wanted to be fed!

After a couple more pups came this way, and Heidi nuzzled and licked them, she understood what was going on—and took charge expertly.

Do you get the parallel?

In Acts nineteen, Paul came upon disciples who'd been dumped, left with no teaching at all about the Holy Spirit. As a result, they were lifeless. He quickly taught them, baptized them in Jesus' name—and wham! they received the Holy Spirit; they inhaled the Holy Breath, and immediately there was glorious new life as the twelve new creatures "spoke with tongues and prophesied." And I can guarantee these transformed disciples felt a new hunger within them for the word—for spiritual food.

See it?

Like Heidi's pup, a new birth can occur without any real evidence of life; it's only as each new creature allows his outer shell to be removed and is encouraged to breathe deeply of the Holy Spirit that stirrings of the inner man can be felt and seen.

So a person can obey Acts 2:38, experience a New birth and become eligible for the precious gift of the Holy Spirit—but if he's never taught to unwrap and *receive* it, he may "lie on the patio in his sack" and waste away!

Unwrap your Gift, dear believer; take off the restrictions of your own will and intellect; receive; "let Him have His way with thee."

This in no way changes the fact that the Bible is our guide and our rock and our source for every principle of life. But how wonderful, how *practical,* to have the Spirit who wrote that book with the hands of men teaching and unfolding it to you!

Jesus and Paul, and Peter, James and John—as well as *most* of those 1st Century disciples—lived in a dimension that included *deed* as well as word, *power* as well as precept (I Corinthians 4:20).

Paul said, "be ye imitators of me as I imitate Christ" which could be interpreted as a pretty conceited thing to say—if you don't understand Paul's recognition of the power of the Holy Spirit in his life.

In my church background, the most quoted scripture would have to be these words of Peter, "Repent, and be baptized every one of you in the name of Jesus Christ for the remission of sins" (Acts 2:38 A.V.). And that's often about as far as we take people; but—that's not all of the verse! There *is* more, and Peter goes on to say, "and ye shall receive the gift of the Holy Ghost."

If you've had occasion to read my book, *A NEW SONG*, you've seen that my own zeal, my great love for Jesus Christ and my desire to share Him with others came only after I had finally individually appropriated this *gift* that God wants every Christian to have.

Just as salvation is individually appropriated—so is the gift of the Holy Spirit.

My emphasis now is on "receiving" rather than giving. Does that sound odd? Well, for so long, I found I had precious little to give *anyone*—other than my own dry concepts and narrow interpretation of the Bible. It was very frustrating that there were few takers.

But John 1:12 has changed that! "But as many as *received* Him, *to them gave He power* to become the sons of God, even to them that believe on His name: which were born, not of blood, nor of the will of the flesh, nor of the will of men, but of God."

Now when I tell people (as God has given the opportunity, often before millions) what I have *received* from God—the very Person and Power of Jesus—people are clamoring to receive from God themselves and He does the giving!

Nobody's ever heard me say that the truths of God's Words are "dull, unsensational and cold"—in fact, they remain as the "unshakeable fact of life." But now for me, there is great new luster and power and depth in those truths since Jesus breathed on me and whispered, "*receive* ye the Holy Ghost." (John 20:22).

It is a gift He gives to every believer, but it *must be received*. "But the man who isn't a Christian can't understand and can't accept these thoughts from God, which the Holy Spirit teaches us. They sound foolish to him, because *only those who have the Holy Spirit within them can understand what the Holy Spirit means.* Others just can't take it in" (I Corinthians 2:14).

21

SPIRITUAL SHERLOCK HOLMES

I am not an authority on anything, and hope never to think of myself as being one.

I want always to be a learner, a searcher, a student of the Word. The apostle Paul spoke of believers as being changed into Jesus' image "from glory to glory even as by the Spirit of the Lord"! (II Corinthians 3:18). Even with all our imperfections and our limited understanding, I believe this is the "birthright of the believer." *Not one of us* is to remain a baby-Christian.

Listen to Paul, the master teacher: "Let us stop going over the same old ground again, and again, always teaching those first lessons about Christ. Let us go on instead to other things and become mature in our understanding, as strong Christians ought to be. Surely we don't need to speak further about the foolishness of trying to be saved by being good, or about the necessity of faith in God; you don't need further instruction about baptism and spiritual gifts and the resurrection of the dead and eternal judgment.

"The Lord willing, we will go on now to other things.

"There is no use trying to bring you back to the Lord again if you have once understood the Good News and tasted for yourself the good things of heaven and shared in the Holy Spirit, and know how good the Word of God is, and felt the mighty powers of the world to come, and then have turned against God. (Hebrews 6:1-5).

I get the distinct idea that Paul expects each of us to "taste of the heavenly gift, to be made partakers of the Holy Ghost, to taste this good Word of God, and the powers of the world to come." What do you make of it?

I detect some hesitancy on your part. Is it because you feel there may be a spiritual Sherlock Holmes lurking in the drawing room curtains—waiting to "expose" your fanaticism if you *do* taste of the heavenly gift? Are you afraid of the consequences from your brethren if you ever *did* become a "partaker of the Holy Ghost"?

Well, I sure can't blame you. I've been there!

It took me long, painful, fruitless years to discover that *each Christian must find, cherish, and develop his own relationship with God through Christ* that is free of undue majority pressure and unfettered by overstrong influence of other individuals. A man can't enjoy the "liberty" for which Christ died if he is afraid to study the Bible for himself and come to some conclusions about worship and service.

If certain individual brethren (who openly affirm that they do *not* have any supernatural help—only their own human intellects) feel empowered to categorically deny and denounce the spiritual experiences and insights of other earnest Christians, then why should the average man waste time studying?

And even more frightening, if these learned men can emphatically declare other dedicated searchers "deceived and deceiving," "false teachers," "unsound," and "definitely" not led by God's Spirit—based completely on their own superior intellectual grasp of the scriptures—well then, the dedicated searcher would do well to put that dangerous Bible aside and just study the books and pronouncements of these learned men.

It's the only "safe" thing to do!

Otherwise, if he comes to his *own* conclusions (and heaven forbid, maybe even has "experiences" in line with those conclusions), and worse still, if he dares to *share* these thoughts and conclusions with other average, ordinary Christians—he will most certainly find himself out of step with the majority, probably discredited and "defused," labeled as "heretic," "wolf in sheep's clothing," "boring from within," "deceiver," "fallen from grace," and eventually disfellowshipped—at least by the learned men and perhaps through *their* influence, by the majority!

Small wonder that many Christians see little point in trying to understand the Bible for themselves today.

Why, a man could find himself "on the outside looking in"!

Yet, I am certain, from my own study, that the Lord will honor and guide the earnest seeker after truth, even if he has only average intelligence and background, limited time and little access to external scholarship.

Jesus pictured us as lambs, sheep, and Himself as the Good Shepherd. I don't find any reference to the need for "sheep dogs," yapping and nipping at the legs of my sheep to keep them in the fold. Jesus says, "My sheep hear My voice"! And it's an apt illustration, I think, that we are pictured as grazing in open pastures, not all chained together or doing the same things at the same time, nor regimented, but free to roam and explore and seek higher ground—yet always listening for the call of the Master's voice. And the sheep, when he hears the Shepherd say, "Come," *obeys,* whether the others do or not. The individual sheep doesn't try to round up the others; he just obeys. And if the others have heard, they do the same thing, coming their own way. Sheep leave the worries of rounding up the "strays" to the Shepherd. There is beauty and freedom, love and trust in the Master in that portrayal.

Oh, I know—and am grateful—that we human "sheep" have been given the opportunity of trying to help our Shepherd round up strays and keep them in the fold. But not with our teeth—"sheep" don't bite. And I'm grateful for minds and scholarship and lives of study and contemplation; they're so valuable and helpful, especially for those who don't have the time and means to do it for themselves.

But, Jesus says, *"My* sheep hear *My* voice!"

I get the distinct impression that He intends to keep on leading, culling out, rounding up, chastising and rewarding—*Himself*. He's the "head"; we're the body— and only individual members at that. *He* will make the judgments, decisions, pronouncements, and He will give the orders. Then it will be Him who shows His divine concern or pleasure with our efforts. I believe my individual focus should be on *Him* through my own study and efforts to know Him, and not on the bleating of the other sheep around me.

Am I a heretic for that?

It's one thing to have strong, scholarly opinions, based on study and prayer, and to share them with others—and even to be concerned, vocally, when others seem to "miss the obvious point." But it's quite another thing to be so infallibly sure that those "obvious points" are THE "sound doctrine" that all who see it another way, or from different experience, can summarily be judged wrong, false, displeasing to God, led by false spirits, and fit to be disfellowshipped.

In the first attitude there is love, concern, brotherly-kindness, and long-suffering. I believe the Spirit can lead in that kind of environment. But in the second there is condemnation, self-righteousness, and Pharisaical legalism; and historically, under those conditions, the unity that we see in the church in Ephesus in Ephesians four, has been hard for even God's Spirit to accomplish.

If only these spiritual detectives had to get a license somewhere!

Oh Lord, please spare us from one more Sherlock Holmes in our midst, one more snarling "sheep dog," nipping at our knees in the name of love!

22

NO TWO-THOUSAND YEAR BARRIER

Our excitement today comes from the discovery that *there is no two-thousand year barrier between the Spirit-filled life in the first century and the same thing today.*

What Christians in the first century experienced with Jesus, *we* are meant to experience today! And if that doesn't make every word of the New Testament vibrate with new life and authority—then nothing will. To me it's no wonder that so many liberal theologians can't make up their minds about what to believe for today and what to disregard as first century "phenomenon." It's been said before, and it's still true—once we start to draw lines according to our own understanding, and decide that certain things were for "then" and others for now—we're in trouble, and will soon have 'a form of Godliness, but denying the power thereof.' (II Timothy 3:5).

In II Corinthians—Paul indicates that we are meant to be *living epistles of Christ,* written "not with ink, but with the Spirit of the living God"! And listen— when the Holy Spirit is writing your life into His continuing story, it makes for pretty exciting reading, and *living!*

No, this is not to say that the written Word no longer holds sufficient excitement nor power enough to accomplish what is needed in an individual's life and ministry; the Word is the seed—it holds life and power —but *only as it is put into action!*

Look at your marriage license; it doesn't make for especially exciting reading, does it? Oh, I'm sure it might, from time to time, as it reminds you of the thrilling relationship and wonderful life-changing experiences that have sprung from its authority. The reason so many people find the Bible dull reading is that they really don't conceive of its dynamic power in our day and with our specific problems.

We, in the church, are described numerous times as the very *bride of Christ;* therefore, this precious Word is truly our *marriage contract,* and far, far more.

In our earthly marriage relationships we know that we are bound to experience emotional ups and downs. In the same way, how can we have a living, breathing relationship as marriage partners with Jesus and not be emotional about real experiences that are bound to spring from a vital union with the very Son of God? In I Corinthians six, Paul admonishes us to "glorify God in your body and spirit!" How could it be any other way if our bodies are actual breathing temples of the "Holy Ghost"? Paul asks, "Haven't you yet learned that your body is the home of the Holy Spirit God gave you, and that he lives within you?" (verse 19).

Of course, if you're not having any experiences with Jesus—well, that's a different matter.

Some folks accuse the Spirit-filled Christian, because of his experience with the Holy Spirit, of denying the "all sufficiency of the Word of God." How I wish you could be in our home just for a little while. You would see our daughters, as well as Shirley and me, devouring the Word like we never did before, loving it, believing it, standing on it and claiming its promises in such a beautiful way!

After all—we don't just believe in the all sufficiency of Scripture when it comes to baptism; we know we're supposed to *experience* it. When it comes to communion, simply a belief in the Scripture is not enough—we're supposed to *experience* it. So it is with singing, praying and serving. These things *do,* the Word declares, and we believe it and try to *do* it. There is action accompanying our belief. All this because the Word says so. Doesn't James say that "faith without works—corresponding action—is dead"?

When Paul said to "earnestly desire the better gifts," we decided this is what we would *do*. Paul says "forbid not to speak in tongues." So we haven't. Paul says in Philippians, that "it is God who works in us both to *will* and to *do* His good pleasure." We've experienced it. The point is that *our experiences,* which we gladly share, *have not taken away from the all sufficiency of the Scriptures* in our lives; and as I look at my dear brothers and sisters who have also experienced this new dimension of Spirit-filled living, I see "turned on" Christians who are deeper into the Word than ever! They live it, breathe it, stake their lives on it. For them, and us, that Bible quivers with life!

As I look at today's young people, too, who are experiencing the reality of Jesus in their lives, I shout again that there is no two-thousand year barrier between what happened to first century Christians and those in the twentieth century. It's *amazing*—to pick up magazines and newspapers—to read of what's happening to these "Jesus People." And they *are* Jesus people, most of them, with all their zealous imperfections. If there could have been a magazine or a newspaper account of what was appening on the day of Pentecost and the months immediately after it—I'll just bet it would have sounded quite a bit like what we are reading and hearing today. Jumbled, mixed up, inaccurately reported, unsettled—but real!

Friend, we're living in an age where God's Spirit is moving—perhaps for the last time—throughout the earth, in much the same way He did in that first century. It's a great time to be alive! These things don't take away from the all-sufficiency of the Scripture; *they validate it* all over again, as God truly confirms His Word *right now* with signs and wonder, just as Jesus said He would in the book of Mark!

It's glorious!

Get in on it!

23

THE SCRIPTURAL PATTERN

Christian people for centuries have been going about as far as they can go under their own steam.

So many of us have done our "dead level best," according to what we've believed "the Scriptural pattern" to be—but there are some things obviously missing. Where is the life, the joy, the power? Where is the dynamic that Christians are supposed to have—and that they *did* have in the first century?

Wasn't that part of the pattern?

I humbly submit from my own bitter experience that the desperate need is for *the whole business to be turned over to the Spirit of God.* How refreshing it is to visit in churches where there is spontaneous singing even before the service begins, for instance, and then again during communion. I've even been to church services where the minister burst into a song midway through his sermon! It was precious, unexpected, spontaneous. It was Spirit-inspired, I felt certain, and believe me, nobody left these churches without having been blessed, fed and nourished for the week to come. It was just beautiful!

I suppose what I am getting at, is that in our careful structuring of things we often close out the possibility that God may have something better in store for us than we could have planned for ourselves.

Is it possible, do you think?

In Acts chapter two, the account is given of the coming of the Holy Spirit upon the believers on the Day of Pentecost. It's a thrilling scene—just where the disciples and the believers were gathered, is not quite certain. It was an upper room, we think, but the place is unimportant; what *is* important, is that God fulfilled His promise, spoken to the disciples on the day of His ascension (Acts 1:8, 9).

Jesus' promise that day was that when the Holy Spirit came upon them, *they would receive power* to testify about Him with tremendous effect.

As the one hundred twenty "Jesus Jews," met together in one place to pray, many of them simple Galilean folk who spoke only their own language, the Bible says, "suddenly there was a sound like the roaring of a mighty windstorm in the skies above them and it filled the house where they were meeting. Then, what looked like flames or tongues of fire appeared and settled on their heads. And everyone present was filled with the Holy Spirit and began speaking in languages they didn't know, for the Holy Spirit gave them this ability" (Acts 2:2-4).

It was a miraculous manifestation of the power of the Holy Spirit literally settling upon each believer. It was a supernatural experience, a "baptismal" blessing which issued forth in conversation and words of praise from the lips of those Christians so that the crowds of people, who came running to see what the roaring in the sky was all about, were suddenly "stunned to hear their own languages being spoken by the disciples." And what were they saying? The Bible records that too. "We all hear these men telling in our own languages about the mighty miracles of God!" (Acts 2:11).

This was not gibberish, (though it may have sounded like it, so many were actually speaking—and hearing) this was spontaneous praise from the innermost parts of those disciples, fashioned by the Spirit of God in a miracle. They were speaking in the foreign languages of those gathered from every corner of the world, and it was about *the wonderful works of God*. It enabled the astonished Jews to hear the message that they needed in order to be saved, and go back to their own far-flung lands and relate the "good news" they were now seeing and hearing. It was a wonderful supernatural plan of the heavenly Father, whereby the gospel story could be given out miraculously on a single day—to hearers from many different nations. It was a fantastic infilling needed by the early Christians to make them into disciples who could witness with power for their Savior.

But the marvelous thing about it is that this gift—the power of the Holy Spirit Himself, was not limited to those gathered that Day of Pentecost. Peter stood up and began shouting to the crowd, "Listen, all of you, visitors and residents of Jerusalem alike! Some of you are saying these men are drunk! It isn't true! It's much too early for that! People don't get drunk by 9 A.M.! No! What you see this morning was predicted by the prophet Joel—'In the last days,' God said, 'I will pour out my Holy Spirit upon all mankind, and your sons and daughters shall prophesy, and your young men shall see visions, and your old men dream dreams. Yes the Holy Spirit shall come upon *all my servants, men and women alike,* and they shall prophesy . . ." (verses 14-18).

And then, at the climax of this first recorded gospel sermon, Peter made this astonishing announcement: "For this promise is unto you, and to your children, and to all that are afar off, *even as many as the Lord our God shall call!"* (verse 39).

This gift is meant for *us today*—for you and me—but first we have to learn to surrender to that Spirit and to let Him take over, and to give up our own mental reins. I think of Jesus converting the water to wine in His first miracle at Cana; remember that it remained water—until *it was poured out!* What we as Christians must learn to do, having been given the gift of the Holy Spirit, *is learn to pour it out* so that the Lord can then perform His supernatural work in and through and for us.

God is doing a mighty thing in the world today, and

I believe that it's because we are now in the final stages of the earth's history. He *is* pouring out His Spirit on all flesh, and because we have "seen and heard" and experienced it, more and more Christians are watching "The Scriptural pattern" of Acts two burst into flame again in these last days.

We too, have been called to carry out the Great Commission in its purest form. To do it, we need the empowering of the Holy Spirit. We need miraculous confirmation. It was God's way in the 1st century—and it's God's way now. He calls you and me, just like He did Peter and Paul. If we're willing to be so used, to allow Him to bathe us in His Spirit, we will see God adding to His body the last of those who are being saved.

We must come to the larger view! We must see that God wants sheep, willing servants, surrendered lives, yielded minds and wills—and that He will orchestrate it all, lead, bless and use *all* of us, if we let Him. We don't have to do it on our own power.

He will do it *through us* if we will just quit trying to control and direct His work ourselves, in our own way, according to our finite concept of His pattern.

He's got the pattern; He made it—and He can fashion the wedding garment Himself, if He finds yielded "cloth" to work with.

24

GHOST WRITER IN THE SKY

There are times when I feel like a ghost writer in the sky! I spend a great amount of time in planes, and much of this book was developed from correspondence and material written on flights.

Recently, I was thinking about how Jesus would come for us through this very sky!

No one knows the day or the hour of Jesus' second coming, but He did say in Matthew's record, that we were to learn the parable of the fig tree. This would give us some "clues" as to His second coming. What in the world was he talking about? "Now learn a lesson from the fig tree. When her branch is tender and the leaves begin to sprout, you know that summer is almost here. Just so, when you see all these things beginning to happen, you can know that my return is near, even at the doors. Then at last, this age will come to its close.

"Heaven and earth will disappear, but my words remain forever. But no one knows the date and hour when the end will be—not even the angels. No, nor even God's Son. Only the Father knows.

"The world will be at ease—banquets and parties and weddings—just as it was in Noah's time before the sudden coming of the flood; people wouldn't believe what was going to happen until the flood actually arrived and took them all away. So shall my coming be.

"Two men will be working together in the fields, and

one will be taken, the other left. Two women will be going about their household tasks; one will be taken, the other left."

So be prepared, for you don't know what day your Lord is coming.

"Just as man can prevent trouble from thieves by keeping watch for them, so you can avoid trouble by always being ready for my unannounced return" (Matthew 24:32-44).

The Lord said that those who were spiritually tuned, whose eyes and ears are open, would be able to see the signs pointing to His return. *I sense His soon coming!* Others do, too. We see evidences, warning signals, indicators all around us. YES, I believe we are accelerating toward the greatest moments in all of history. We still don't know the day or the hour—but the Lord intended us to be able to sense the expectancy of all creation, and there are many of us who are doing that very thing. We are waiting expectantly.

Then why are many religious leaders—men, who should be "in-the-know"—scoffing at this growing expectancy and stoutly denying that the Holy Spirit is showering First Century Spiritual gifts on humble Christians? How could this be? Let me share something with you.

As I review what happened on the Day of Pentecost I see something a little more clearly now than I ever have before. What happened there was not just a miracle of utterance, but also a miracle of *hearing*. Those who were speaking obeyed the impulse of the Holy Spirit and "spake as the Spirit gave utterance." That was one miracle. But the Holy Spirit performed another miracle in the ears of those who heard, because (Acts 2:6) "every man (singular) heard them (plural) speak in his (singular) own language." With perhaps 120 people speaking and praising God at once, every man was hearing what they said *in his own language* (verse 8). The account doesn't say that one of the disciples was speaking Parthian, and another the language of the Medes and another the Elamites and so on (although, they may have been); it *does* say that each of those who were hearing with any spiritual discernment was hearing what *they* said in *his* own language.

The sad part is that in verse 13, we see that there were others standing by mocking and picking these things to pieces, seeing no spiritual significance at all in the miracles that were happening right before their eyes!

We see this same spiritual blindness elsewhere in the New Testament. In John eleven, when Jesus knew that Lazarus was sick, he said, "This sickness is not unto death, but for the glory of God, that the Son of God might be glorified thereby" (verse 4). Jesus intended for the death and subsequent resurrection of Lazarus to bring glory to His Father, to bear witness to His own ministry, and to bring about belief *in those who perceived* the spiritual significance of what happened. But what really did happen? After this fantastic deed was done, in John 11:47 through 53, we see the religious leaders of Jesus' day "convening a council to discuss the situation" (verse 47), plotting to eradicate the Son of God Himself, in spite of the fact that they had to admit that "this man certainly does miracles."

Why should they want to do away with Jesus? Because He was rocking their doctrine, disputing their positions of leadership, endangering their position in their own brotherhood, and even posing a threat to their national security. *They saw no spiritual significance* in what Jesus was doing, only a threat to their cherished doctrines and status.

Then in the twelfth chapter of John we read how these same religious leaders decided they must also put *Lazarus* to death, because he was walking proof of Jesus' teaching and miracle-working power! Ordinary people were "flocking to see him" (verse 9), and even many Jewish leaders were deserting their traditional beliefs and believing instead in Jesus. Again, these chief priests and Pharisees who plotted against Jesus couldn't be concerned with the spiritual reality before their very eyes, but were only concerned with eradicating that which posed as a threat to long established doctrine and position.

110

In Acts, the eighth chapter, we see the brilliant, zealous, educated and self-righteous Saul actively persecuting innocent Spirit-filled disciples. He was convinced that he was doing God's work—though he was using man's methods and throwing men and women into prison with what almost seems like ferocious glee. You and I read that now, and wonder *how anybody could have been so blind.* Why couldn't Paul (then called Saul) *see,* and why couldn't the chief priests, the scribes and Pharisees *see,* that Jesus was the Son of God and that His Holy Spirit had been given in miraculous measure to His disciples?

Isn't it interesting that the ones who were doing the persecuting and leading in this rebellion against God and the move of His Spirit were the Old Testament scholars, the Ph.D.s, the religious leaders and the intellectual giants of their day? Isn't it interesting that Jesus purposely chose lowly and uneducated men, for the most part, as His apostles? Isn't it interesting that the great majority of those who followed Jesus, and saw His spiritual dominion, were common and ordinary people, without much education? Isn't it interesting that Jesus Himself thanked His Father intimately for *hiding* these things from the wise and prudent—and *revealing* them unto "babes"? (Matthew 11:25, 26). Isn't it also highly dramatic that Paul, after his miraculous and supernatural encounter with the living Jesus, drew attention to the fact that "not many wise men after the flesh, not many mighty, not many noble, are called" (I Corinthians 1:26)? There was recognition on the part of Paul that already, in his day, few who follow Christ have big names or power or wealth. "Instead," he says, "God has deliberately chosen to use ideas the world considers foolish and of little worth *in order to shame those people considered by the world as wise and great.* He has chosen a plan despised by the world, counted as nothing at all, and used it to bring down to nothing those the world considers so great, so that no one anywhere can ever brag in the presence of God."

Isn't it interesting that Saul himself, reduced from his lofty intellectual position to that of a blind helpless

111

beggar, had to be ministered to by Ananias, about whom we know nothing except that he was "a disciple," a follower of Jesus? Isn't it interesting that God loved him enough to cripple him physically and allow him to be afflicted materially and physically for the rest of his life—to bring him into a place of submission and true spiritual light? There was no other way, because Saul was determined, like Adam, that *his brain must rule his spirit*.

Man was not created for this, and God has suffered long with us to bring our spirits back into authority over our brains. Ever since Eden, man has wanted it the other way around, at the insidious prompting of Satan.

How it must have "bugged" the Devil then, when he saw Jesus walking down into the river Jordan—to be baptized by John the Baptist! Why was He doing that? Jesus had no sin—Satan had been unable to soil Him once! Then why—*why?* It made no sense; it was "foolish"!

Right?

Jesus' perfect intellect was being programmed by His yielded spirit. He wasn't doing things that necessarily "made sense" to His mind. He was just "taking orders"; He said flatly in John 5:30, "I can of mine own self do nothing! As I hear, I judge; and my judgment is just because *I seek not my own will*, but the will of the Father which hath sent me."

So, when John saw Jesus standing before him, he said, in effect, "Hey—what *is* this? You're not a sinner. You're the Lamb of God who will take away the sins of the world! You should baptize me! This is backwards! It's not reasonable, it's not rational—it's—well, it's *foolish*, that's what it is!"

And what did Jesus say, so quietly? "Suffer it to be so now; for thus it becometh us to fulfill all righteousness."

Us!

He was saying, in effect, "I know, John, this isn't rational, and it does seem backward—maybe even foolish. But my Father wants me to do this. And He wants *you* to do it, too. Isn't that enough? Does it have to make sense to our minds? Let's just obey God, you and I, and my Father will declare us righteous, because we do what He says, whether it appeals to our intellects or not."

And you know what? John baptized Jesus—and the heavens opened, and God poured His Holy Spirit on His yielded Son right on the spot!

Your Father and mine was so thrilled to see His Jesus simply obeying Him, bending His mind to His spirit—that He shouted His Almighty pleasure from heaven!

I want to be like Jesus. I want to please my Father by obeying Him. He gave me a wonderful brain—but if that brain isn't programmed by His spirit, yielded to His will, I can't please Him. He deliberately chooses foolish things for me to do—to check me out, to see whether my mind is controlling my actions—or His Spirit.

He did it with Jesus, and He'll do it with you.

He's coming soon. And this "ghost writer in the sky" is planning to be one of those who rises to meet Him in the air.

I *know* it doesn't make sense!

You can stay here and figure it all out, if you want to—I'm getting ready to fly!

25

ONCE I WAS BLIND, BUT NOW I CAN SEE!

Can you imagine trying to persuade Cornelius (Acts 10) or the Christians mentioned in Acts nineteen that they had *not* received the Holy Spirit?

Paul's very first question to those Ephesian disciples was, "Did you receive the Holy Spirit when you believed?" (Acts 19:2).

"No," they replied, "we don't know what you mean. What is the Holy Spirit?" Paul had already sensed a lack of power and direction in these disciples—and he diagnosed the problem immediately! There was obviously something lacking in their knowledge, their obedience and their experience. So, he told them about Jesus, and probably included something like Peter did in Acts 2:38, because: "As soon as they heard this, they were baptized in the name of the Lord Jesus. Then when Paul laid his hands upon their heads, *the Holy Spirit came on them,* and they spoke in other languages and prophesied. The men involved were about twelve in number."

As I read this I wonder again how so many of us could deny that believers today are to receive the Holy Spirit. Notice again that *this was Paul's first question* to these men! But then I remember that I lived for thirty years on the other side of the Baptism in the Holy Spirit—and I remember being totally blind to all passages of scripture, like Acts 19, which obviously offer this experience and dimension of life to every disciple of Jesus. I often used this passage to point out the necessity of *water* baptism; but the equally essential authorization for *Spirit* baptism seemed to vanish before my eyes!

In John's gospel there's the story of the blind beggar whom Jesus miraculously healed. This "impossible" event really shook the neighbors, the community—and the religious leaders—who had known him all his life as a blind beggar. In fact, they asked the question, "Is this the same fellow—that beggar?" (John 9:8).

"Some said yes, and some said no. 'It can't be the same man,' they thought, 'but he surely looks like him!'

"And the beggar said, 'I *am* the same man!'

"Then they asked him how in the world he could see. What had happened?

"And he told them, 'A man they call Jesus made mud and smoothed it over my eyes and told me to go to the Pool of Siloam and wash off the mud. I did, and I can see!'

" 'Where is he now?' they asked.

" 'I don't know,' he replied.

"Then they took the man to the Pharisees."

The Pharisees, of course, were panicked; but they pretended their concern was over the fact that the miracle had occurred on the Sabbath. The blind man's parents were called in to confirm the fact that this was their son, and that, yes, he had been *born* blind. But they, in fear of being excommunicated, refused to confirm the story of the miraculous healing! "We don't know what happened to make him see, or who did it. He is old enough to speak for himself. Ask him," they said fearfully.

Their attitude is a curious, sad commentary on the power of religious intimidation. Cowering in the presence of the livid Pharisees, the parents "pleaded the 5th amendment" when they should have been almost delirious with excitement and praise.

But, can you imagine trying to persuade their son that he was somehow deluded into just "thinking" that

115

he could see? The Jewish leaders called the man in "for the second time and told him, 'Give the glory to God, not to Jesus, for we know Jesus is an evil person.' "

The man's answer is so eloquent in its simplicity: "I don't know whether he is good or bad," the man replied, "but I know this: *I was blind, and now I see!*"

Hard to argue with that, isn't it?

The once blind man didn't give them some nice philosophical lecture on their doctrinal differences, but boldly upbraided them for their unreasonable opposition to the evidence of the miracle that the man Jesus had performed. He, who was the recipient of the power and grace of the Lord Jesus, stood marveling at the willfulness of those who were determined to reject Him. He was amazed that they couldn't see with their own eyes that this Man had to be from God—and he openly argued with them. He defended with great zeal the honor of Christ, and his own experience at His hands, not caring what this might do to his standing within the Temple.

"Look!" the man exclaimed. "I told you once; didn't you listen? Why do you want to hear it again? Do you want to become His disciples too?"

Of course that infuriated the "righteous" leaders and they cursed him and said, *"You* are His disciple, but we are disciples of *Moses.* We know God has spoken to Moses, but as for this fellow, we don't know anything about him."

"Why, that's very strange" the man replied. "He can heal blind men, and yet you don't know anything about him! Well, God doesn't listen to evil men, but He has open ears to those who worship Him and do His will. Since the world began there has never been anyone who could open the eyes of someone born blind. If this man were not from God, He couldn't do it." This man could see the facts clearly, they were simple to him.

All of this resulted in the leaders throwing the man out of the Temple. This isn't strange nor unusual; I've heard of similar things being done yet today. It's always easier to dismiss as "heresy" or "self-delusion" miracles and transformations which one cannot deny or explain!

But a sweet and wonderful thing happened next.

Jesus Himself sought out the lonely outcast and led him into still more light. The one who had wrought the miracle now revealed Himself as the very Son of God. Look at the end of this true story with me: the scene closes with the once-blind man worshipping Jesus as his Messiah. In painful contrast stand the Pharisees. With their "superior intellect," with all their doctrinal purity and knowledge of the scriptures, they stand condemned.

I'm just sure that many times in the days afterward, the happy man must have shaken his head and wondered, "How can they that see, *not* see?"

The Bible speaks of this Spiritual myopia in many places. Paul, in Ephesians, makes mention of those whose understanding is darkened, alienated from the life of God through the willful ignorance that is in them, because of the blindness and the hardness of their hearts.

Jesus speaks of them as the "blind leading the blind" (Matthew 15:15). And in John's gospel, chapter twelve, we can listen to the Lord Himself talking about the Light shining in the darkness: "My light will shine out for you just a little while longer," Jesus says to the crowd. "Walk in it while you can, and go where you want to go before the darkness falls, for then it will be too late for you to find your way. Make use of the Light while there is still time; then you will become light bearers. . . . I have come as a Light to shine in this dark world, so that all who put their trust in me will no longer wander in the darkness" (verses 35, 36, 46).

Jesus is the Master Optometrist.

Only He can open blind eyes. Only He can perform spiritual open-heart surgery—and even transplant a new one for the old! Even his spit, mixed with dust, can open deaf ears and blind eyes!

What was the matter with those "religious" guys? They knew the Bible, didn't they? Sure they did.

117

They were good moral people, weren't they? I imagine so.

Didn't they pray, and tithe, and teach Sunday school? Why, I'll bet they did.

What was wrong then?

They didn't know Jesus.

They were so busy doing the "right" things; preserving the status quo; deciding who was acceptable to God, and forming iron-clad opinions on every religious matter—that when the Son of God walked into their midst and performed incredible miracles right before them, all they could think about was how this man in His power was challenging their very lives!

They couldn't see that's *why He came:* to challenge, and change, and uproot, and transform and shake up and cast down and frighten people to death—and back into life everlasting.

He sure did it to me. I stand with you, nameless Christian brother of John nine. All I really know is—"I was blind, but now I can see."

26

ROCKING THE BOAT

The religious leaders of Jesus' day, to put it in twentieth century language, were very much afraid of "rocking the boat" or of "having the boat rocked" by Jesus and His followers. Things haven't changed too much in the intervening centuries, have they?

We read in the gospel of John that "even many of the Jewish leaders believed Jesus to be the Messiah but wouldn't admit it to anyone because of the fear that the Pharisees would excommunicate them from the synagogue; *for they loved the praise of men more than the praise of God.*" If that's not the same as saying they were afraid of "rocking the boat," I don't know what would be!

There are some of us who, in our search for deeper spirituality, more complete commitment to the leadership of Christ, happier fuller relationships with the Savior, have set about to re-examine the Scriptures to determine the total will of God. There are home Bible studies going on all over the country (and the world), and ordinary people are buying Bibles, reading and discussing excitedly with others—outside of "church"! Some are actually reporting miraculous, supernatural experiences with Jesus! And all of this strange activity is "rocking the boat" where church leaders gather.

Should we all just settle back complacently and assume that somebody with a Ph.D. already knows all there is to know about God's will—that the studying has been done for us, the questions all answered, all issues settled—and that it's pointless for us to seek any more of the Lord in our lives than others have experienced? I've raised the question before; the answer always comes back "Yes"—if we're afraid of open discussion, of maybe new "discovery," of possible controversy, of some over-eagerness and even some human error (as if this were new) in the enthusiasm of the study. "Yes"—if acceptance by the majority is the prime concern. Nobody likes to think that he's missed some truth along the way; even to bring up *questions* is enough to nettle many.

So, if we're afraid of "rocking the boat"—and maybe getting thrown overboard in the process, like Jonah—the answer to the above questions has to be "Yes"!

We *should* just sit down and do as we're told.

But wait—that boat Jonah was in was being "rocked," and Jonah *did* get thrown overboard—precisely because he *wanted* to just sit down and shut up! He didn't want to speak out! He wanted to let the people of Nineveh shift for themselves; he didn't want to be involved in unpopular controversy, to be the object of scorn and rejection, to say things that could only make him unwelcome to the majority! So Jonah tried ducking out, dodging responsibility, ignoring the leading, yes, the very voice, of God!

But the boat "got rocked" anyway!

And God's will got done anyway!

Doesn't our boat, the Church, need some rocking today?

Don't we *need* new study, new zeal, fresh examination, new urgency for the gigantic tasks that face us? Haven't we been settling into self-satisfied complacency even while millions of young people have been "deserting the ship" in their own search for new life, and while drastic storms are starting to break all around us? While the evangelistic fervent tidal wave of atheistic Communism sweeps over the world, and torrents of perversion, immorality, pornography, rebellion and an-

120

archy, humanism, mysticism, violence, drugs, astrology, occult worship, witchcraft and counterfeit religions—and even the open worship of Satan threaten to drown us all?

More than ever, it seems essential that we "put on the whole armor of God, that we may be able to stand against the wiles of the devil"! It *is* a spiritual battle we're in and Satan is on the rampage! I don't think we're going to win the fight and convert the world (or even our own young people *within* the church, let alone out there in the world), with a dry appeal to the intellect, with a "pat" set of rules. The gale is howling, the waves are pitching high, and people—individuals—are adrift in a raging sea.

I believe God is calling people together, telling us to quit looking at our differences and each put on our life jackets—individually—and let the Master of Earth and Sky take the helm! We need His Spirit *in* us and *through* us all!

And He moves best through yielded souls, reaching out to others, motivated by love, and shouting *encouragements* to those still adrift and struggling to get on board—not through would-be "Captain Blighs" who try to cast off those who don't "look right," who have their hats on crooked, or who perchance happen to see things from a different perspective than we do!

For too long we've been trying to decide for ourselves who is pleasing to God and who isn't, and thus the barriers have grown between us, as we've tried to sort things out intellectually. There's no time for that now; we'd better be letting the "unity of the Spirit" show through us as *God* does the choosing of who's pleasing to Him and who is not! If we implore Him to help us see ourselves and remove the beams in our *own* eyes, we may discover, with new vision, that He's been busy doing the same for others—*without our scalpels!*

Paul says that we are *not* to esteem ourselves better than others (Philippians 2:3). We have so often taken the directly opposite approach: we *have* esteemed ourselves better than others. Strife and vainglory have abounded, just as the Word said it would happen. Yes, we have felt we were "defending the doctrine," and in some instances, I believe we *have* been; but from this sense of "rightness" has come a feeling and an air of superiority which has a negative effect on others. Instead of letting God show others His will, perhaps through our example and manner of life—especially loving humility—we've tried to bind others to our concepts, right or wrong; and we've judged, condemned and excluded others if they don't agree with us.

Paul says this judging business is up to God, not us, and we only succeed in erecting barriers and driving people *away* from the Light of the truth, when *we* try to do it!

In I Corinthians 2 verse 5 we are told that *our faith should not stand in the widsom of men, but in the power of God.* Disastrous suffocating results occur when we operate in the reverse of that.

Jonah's self-protective silence as he sailed to Tarshish caused God to rock the boat to such an extent that Jonah *had* to be thrown overboard. But it was this very thing that caused the men in the ship to stand in awe before Jehovah, and sacrifice to Him and vow to serve Him (Jonah 1:16).

The Lord is still rocking boats. He has to.

And, though the turbulence often focuses around an individual, God's purpose is to shake *everybody* up! Thank God, He loves us enough to throw us overboard and have some of us swallowed by big fishes of calamity, trial and persecution! If, in the process, others stand in awe before Him, and find Him in a new and vital way, and then vow to serve Him the rest of their lives, —we can only say, "Praise the Lord!" Keep on rocking the boat, Master!

Shake us up good!

And your will be done in all things!

27

PRAYER: SUPERNATURAL OR PSYCHOLOGICAL?

I'd like to "rock" you now with the choice that got me thrown overboard ("disfellowshipped") from my life-long church brotherhood! I'd stayed meek and quiet for many years, ignoring the voice of God. Whenever this choice would arise, I'd quickly "table" it, because I knew the "wrong" (right?) answer would run counter to our long-established doctrine. But, finally I had to face it—and so do you. It's this: *prayer is either supernatural or psychological!*

There can be no middle ground. Either we expect God to step in and change things that otherwise would have occurred "naturally"—or we don't! If the "effectual, fervent prayer of righteous man availeth much"—if it even availeth anything—how does it happen?

Think about it, now. Think about the fervent prayer of a righteous man—.

Does this kind of praying bring about change in the normal, "natural" course of things? If not—why pray?

Or does God hear, decide, and step across His own natural law (including the law of cause and effect) to change what otherwise would have happened "naturally"? If we believe the latter, we believe in the *super-natural*, in Divine intervention, in God suspending the natural course in answer to the prayer of His children. If we pray for God to help the preacher, the elders, the sick person, the wayward child, the financial problem—whatever—we're asking Him to change what otherwise would have happened, according to natural law! And that's *super*natural!

Once we realize and accept that, our pulse quickens. "With God, nothing is impossible." (Matthew 17:20) As sons of God, joint heirs with Christ, with the very angels as our ministering servants we can be more bold in our prayers, our faith can grow to greater dimensions, our confidence in His nearness and power can quicken our response to Him! Yes, we must pray according to the knowledge of His will, but there is suddenly a greater desire to understand what is His will. It's exciting!

One of the major reasons most of us have had such a shallow religious experience is that we have tried to do away, consciously or subconsciously, with the supernatural in our relationship to God. We keep saying that God does answer prayer—but that He does it "through natural means."

Now get this: if God does not suspend His natural law in order to answer our prayers, we are then in effect saying that prayer is wholly psychological, and self-contained. I repeat, if our Lord doesn't block what was going to happen (before we prayed), and change things supernaturally to meet our request; if what we asked for was going to happen anyway, naturally—why pray? Save your breath!

But if we do believe that God actually hears the prayer of a man, and steps in to answer that prayer, then we believe that He is suspending and cutting across what otherwise would have happened according to His natural law. *At whatever point* the hand of God actually changes things, He has moved in a *supernatural* way—He has suspended His own natural principles, including the scientific law of cause and effect.

In fact, if God even *hears* our prayers—*that's* supernatural! What "natural" law does *that* conform to?

I get letters all the time from people who say, "I guess it's only *natural* that my minister and others cannot understand and accept my relationship and experience as being from God." How true this really is! For Paul, an intellectual giant himself, says that "the natural man cannot comprehend the things of the Spirit." (I Corinthians 2:14) And Paul was talking about *Christians!* As long as man reasons with his mind only, he cannot even imagine the overwhelming love of God.

I once heard a radio minister ask, "Why didn't God say 'Behold, I stand at your *mind* and knock?' "

There are so many scriptural references about receiving Christ into the heart. "For salvation that comes from trusting Christ—which is what we preach—is already within easy reach of each of us; in fact, is as near as our own hearts and mouths. For if you tell others with your own mouth that Jesus Christ is your Lord, and believe in your own heart that God has raised Him from the dead, you will be saved. *For it is by believing in his heart* that a man becomes right with God; and with his mouth he tells others of his faith, confessing his salvation."

How does a man believe with his heart? Does Paul mean "mind"? No.

Our minds intellectualize and rationalize and often block the heart from receiving unreservedly the *supernatural* manifestation of God's love—whether that manifestation is some specific answer to prayer, receiving some special "gift" from Him, or whatever.

God wants me to accept Him with my whole being —and not just the intellectual part of my being. Jesus said He wants to come in and sup with me, to dwell intimately with me! (Revelations 3:20 and John 14:23).

In our own daily lives, my family and I have seen and experienced many *supernatural* things, including healing and answered prayer of many kinds. The natural reaction of most "church folks," as it was mine before I began to understand the power of the Holy Spirit, is to try and figure out how these answered prayers, for instance, might somehow have been psychologically induced, or whether they are just "coincidence," or perhaps wholly imaginary.

What does this kind of response say about our attitude toward prayer itself, and our relationship with God?

Paul said to *"thank God for everything,"* and that love "hopeth all things, *believeth all things,* endureth all things" (I Corinthians 13). I have found there is more power for Christian living and witnessing in giving God credit for answering prayer and for changing things, than there ever *will* be in trying to rationally "explain things." I've *been* one of those watery rationalists who looks for every explanation under the sun to avoid just admitting that God has performed a supernatural miracle!

I understand more now what Paul meant when he said that "hope maketh not ashamed; and we feel this warm love everywhere within us because *God has given us the Holy Spirit to fill our hearts with His love"* (Romans 5:5).

I no longer have any trouble accepting the fact that God moves in supernatural ways to answer prayer; nor that the gift of His Holy Spirit is a supernatural manifestation of His love. Jesus Himself gave us such an easy-to-understand picture of this very thing—knowing, as He did, how the human mind works—when He said, "You men who are fathers—if your boy asks for bread, do you give him a stone? If he asks for fish, do you give him a snake? If he asks for an egg, do you give him a scorpion? Of course not!

"And if even sinful persons like yourselves give children what they need, don't you realize that your heavenly Father will do at least as much, and *give the Holy Spirit to those who ask for Him?* (Luke 11:11-13).

Doe He do that?

Or doesn't He?

Careful, now. If you answer "yes; I believe God's word. I believe God will do exactly what He says,"— you may be letting yourself in for trouble.

Unless you just settle for some safe, sensible "mind trip" (which is the same as saying "No—I don't believe God means what He says")—you may start to experience supernatural things in your life and miraculous answers to your prayers.

Why, the Lord may even *manifest Himself to you,* as He says in John 14:21!

But think about it. You may be "disfellowshipped," smirked about, ostracized, gossiped over and whispered right out of your church group. You just might find yourself "on the outside looking in."

Just you—and Jesus.

Think it over!

28

TWO SPIRITUAL POWERS AT WORK

Almost all of the practices of the first century Church were duplicated and counterfeited in pagan religions.

They baptized (and do today even in witchcraft), they had different kinds of singing and worship, they claimed miracles and healing and signs and wonders. And still today all these things are being practiced by those who do not know the power of the Holy Spirit. Actually these same things testify to the reality of Jesus and His ministry—*when God's power* is in them.

So what's the answer? It's obvious; and it's biblical: *there are two spiritual powers at work in the world*. This book concerned itself with the thunder of the Holy Spirit's power. But Satan's power is incredibly real too, second only to that of the Lord Himself.

I have never yet heard a minister of the gospel affirm that Satan stopped *his* supernatural working in the first century. Those of us who have done some mortal combat with the devil know something of the devious way he works. But one look around you in the world today is convincing proof that Satanic force is hard at work. Of course, Paul *said* the devil and his angels were waging war on Christians, in Ephesians 6:10-13; but that was so long ago, wasn't it?

The Bible shows that Satan's principal concern is to do battle with the followers of Christ. I often say that the devil already *has* the world deceived, so he doesn't need to concern himself as much with them; but it's the saints of Jesus that could give him trouble—so he gives us "both barrels"! He *knows* that the best defense is a good offense; and we let him do it to us all the time.

In Luke's gospel, for instance, we see Jesus coming down from the mount of transfiguration where the disciples had witnessed that breaktaking scene—Moses and Elijah, in person, speaking to Jesus about what would happen to Him at Jerusalem! When they descended from that mountaintop experience, a huge crowd met them, and a man came running out of the crowd. We have reason to believe that he was a follower of Jesus for he called out, "Teacher, Master, this boy here is my only son, and a demon keeps seizing him making him scream; and it throws him into convulsions so that he foams at the mouth; it is always hitting him and hardly ever leaves him alone. I begged your disciples to cast the demon out, but they couldn't" (Luke 9:38-40).

What a stark picture of life's elemental conflict this is! Just hours before, Jesus and the disciples had been encompassed by the very glories of heaven—and now, once more, here they are surrounded by the demonic realities and suffering of earth. In each of these confrontations (there were many of them faithfully recorded in the gospels) the compassion of the Father-heart of God, shining through His Son, completely vanquished the perverted power of darkness and evil.

Immediately, Jesus was moved with tender pity as he heard the agonizing words of the father and saw the distress of the demon-possessed son. He said, "Bring him to me." Jesus never hesitated in the presence of human need, and, Praise God, He has not changed today! That same mighty power is available to *us* if we approach Him in faith, like that helpless father.

Jesus healed that boy by ordering the demon to come out of him. His power, motivated by love, is greater than the supernatural mighty power of Satan: and it's the only power *that is!* When the boy was healed, Jesus handed him over to his father—and "awe

129

gripped the people as they saw *this display of the power of God."*

I really believe the Lord would like each of us to be filled with genuine awe in His presence—and often. But instead, we question those whom God is using in awesome ways. I think of my good friends, Charles and Frances Hunter, whose lives have been magnificently touched by God and through whom His power is being demonstrated in ways that are right out of the books of Acts. (Read their two latest books—at the time of this writing—*Two Sides of a Coin* and *Since Jesus Passed By.*) Yes unbelievers ridicule what God is doing in the lives of others whom the Holy Spirit is using.

I believe it is safe to say that Satan is now pulling out all the stops in contending with the saints—blinding minds, sowing discord, strifes, hatred, and division —with a vengeance! An acquaintance told me recently that while she was reading the Hunters' book *Since Jesus Passed By* in the beauty shop, a Christian friend asked to look at it; so she gave it to her. This friend later gave it back to her with the comment, "We're just on different spiritual wave lengths." And she had said it perfectly! The implication was clear—the friend neither believed nor understood this display of the power of God working through the Hunters. They *are* on different spiritual wave lengths! Satan is having a field-day!

Satan is a deceiver. Satan is the accuser of our brethren. In Revelation twelve, the great war in heaven is chronicled, in which Michael and the angels under his command fought the Dragon and his hosts of fallen angels, but the Dragon prevailed not; that is, he lost the battle and was forced from heaven. "This great Dragon —the ancient serpent called the devil, or Satan, *the one deceiving the whole world*—was thrown down *onto the earth* with all his army." And then we hear the "Woe." "But woe to you people of the world, for the devil has come down to you in great anger, knowing that he has little time."

And friend, dear brother or sister—the war is on.

How do we overcome this deceiver? Over and over

again the Bible tells us *our weapon is love*—love of Christ and love for the brethren. We're meant to be walking epistles of love with joined hearts, hands and minds. We're *not* meant to be on "different spiritual wave lengths."

The Bible talks about *one believer* being able to rout a thousand demons—and two *ten thousand!* Small wonder that Satan puts "sowing discord among brethren" at the top of his list of tactical priorities! It's his major defense!

And didn't Jesus send His disciples out "two by two"?

Could it be that Paul stressed "unity in the Spirit in the bond of love" (Ephesians 4) for this reason? I think so—because, in that great plea for singlemindedness he explains the source of Spiritual gifts, the duration (till *we all come* in the unity of the faith)—and the purpose of them: to bring us, the body of Christ, to *His full stature!*

Then, Satan—*look out!*

Look back at the story of Jesus and the demon-possessed boy; you see the twisted supernatural power of the Devil, ruining the body and the soul of even a child. Now look around you at our world today; observe young people swept up into the use of mind-altering drugs, their bodies being ravaged, their minds being possessed through occult fascinations, and their very souls destroyed. Can't you see how relentless Satan is in his demonic plan to control the minds and hearts of the world's young? Listen—if they're ever to be rescued from eternal destruction, it will come only as they see *the supernatural power of God at work* through Spirit-filled Christians who are not wasting their time and energies devouring and fighting each other—but are joining forces to squash the Devil. No dry doctrinal preachment can reclaim them now.

In the Old Testament we get several glimpses of Satan as the accuser, contending with saints. In Zechariah three, Joshua the High Priest stands before the angel of the Lord with Satan *right there,* resisting and accusing him! (vs 1). "And the Lord said to Satan, "I *reject* your accusations, Satan; yes, I, the Lord—I rebuke you" (vs. 2). And this stands for all time as an example to all who would live a victorious life in Christ!

How do we overcome Satan as accuser? (—and have you never felt him accusing you of failure, of worthlessness, of hypocrisy, of faithlessness?) You'd better not try it with your mind—it'll let you down. You'd better not depend on your doctrinal "rightness" —all have sinned, and fallen short. *BE FILLED WITH THE SPIRIT!* Invite that *ONE* to fill you who can stand before the devil and strike terror in his black heart: "Get thee hence, Satan, for it is written, Thou shalt not tempt the Lord thy God" (Matthew 4:1-10).

If you dare try to face the supernatural tests of Satan without the miraculous power of the Holy Spirit—you are a ludicrous, vanquished foe.

Christ submitted to His temptation by Satan—He walked out into the wilderness, fasted for days—and cut old Beelzebub to bits with the Word! He faced that showdown so that He might show God's mighty power on His and our behalf. And He did it! Through Him, Paul says, we too are more than conquerors. But *how* did He do it, in His weakened condition? With his intellect? His grasp of the scriptures alone? No, He was *"led by the Spirit"* (Matthew 4:1).

And Paul says ". . . your strength must come from *the Lord's mighty power within you"* (Ephesians 6:10)!

Now, that Christian who sets himself to be led of God's Spirit can expect to be the special object of vicious assault by Satan—just as Jesus was. He will be accused, abused and refused. He will face temptations of ego, of greed and power—and self-destruction. Just as Jesus did.

What's the answer? To seek the Lord *in Spirit and in Truth;* to put on *the whole armor* to proclaim the full gospel (Mark 16; 15-18)—and "be strengthened *with might by His Spirit* in the inner man"! (Ephesians 3:16).

132

Don't face a supernatural enemy with human resources!

What folly to attempt an intellectual defense against this corruption, when part of the demonic power of Satan is blinding minds: "If the Good News we preach is hidden to anyone, it is hidden from the one who is on the road to eternal death. *Satan, who is the god of this evil world, has made him blind,* unable to see the glorious light of the Gospel that is shining upon him, *or to understand the amazing message we preach* about the glory of Christ, who is God. We don't go around preaching about ourselves, but about Christ Jesus as Lord. . . . For God, who said, 'Let there be light in the darkness,' has made us understand that it is the brightness of His glory that is seen in the face of Jesus Christ.

"But this precious treasure—this light and power that now shine within—is held in a perishable container, that is, in our weak bodies. Everyone can see that *the glorious power within must be from God and is not our own*" (2 Corinthians 4: 3-7, itals. author's).

A sign—a wonder, a manifestation—of Satan's power in the world today is the universal blindness to his reality! He's done his work well, convincing even Christians—even ministers and theologians—that he no longer walks the earth as a roaring lion (I Peter 5:8). I've heard in horror, from the lips of church elders, that "There's doubt about a real Satan" while their own children are being lured away!

Still, because this blindness to spiritual reality is Satanic in origin and grip—Paul says it's useless to argue about it. Satan *loves* an argument! Listen: "Don't get involved in foolish arguments which only upset people and make them angry. God's people must not be quarrelsome; they must be gentle, patient teachers of those who are wrong. Be humble when you are trying to teach those who are mixed up concerning the truth. For if you talk meekly and courteously to them they are more likely, with God's help, to turn away from their wrong ideas and believe what is true. *Then they will come to their senses and escape from Satan's trap of slavery to sin which he uses to catch them whenever he likes, and then they can begin doing the will of God"* (2 Timothy 2:23-26).

There are two powerful spiritual forces clashing head-on in the world today. And we're in the middle, like it or not. We have the right to ask God's Spirit, Who authored His Word, to help us, supernaturally, to come to the understanding of the Bible that He wants us to have. That mighty Word is our weapon in this warfare—but it's the Sword *of the Spirit!* It's only as we rely upon God's *supernatural power given through His Holy Spirit* that we can be overcomers.

But we *can* overcome! We *can* "resist the devil" and see him flee! We *can* "bruise his head"—but only as we submit to the total dominance of Jesus, the Lord, filling our flesh, our minds, our souls.

Can you hear that beloved John's assurance? "Greater is *He that is in you,* than he that is in the world" (I John 4:4).

29

THE GREAT GIFT OF LOVE

Are the gifts of the Spirit really important in the 20th Century?

Wasn't all that stuff just some mysterious "mumbo-jumbo" to get the church going in the beginning? Didn't the Holy Spirit just sort of shoot off some fireworks to launch this new thing on the earth? Those charismatic things weren't meant to just keep going, on and on—*were* they?

God knew there would be misunderstanding about the supernatural work of the Spirit, so He moved upon the apostle Paul to write specifically about it. Paul says, "for I don't want any misunderstanding about them." (I Corinthians 12:1).

In fact, three chapters in first Corinthians are devoted to an in-depth teaching on the work and gifts of the Holy Spirit in the church—more than you'll find in any one place on communion, baptism, giving or any other single activity of believers in the whole New Testament.

In Chapter twelve, Paul talks about these abilities as individual gifts, which the Holy Spirit alone distributes to those who can be entrusted with them. In chapter thirteen, he says that even if a person had *all* these supernatural gifts, and didn't have a God-given love operating through them, they wouldn't profit anybody much. (This was actually the case in the church at Corinth to which he was writing.) And then, in the fourteenth chapter, he gives detailed instruction about "speaking in tongues" since this was probably the most common of the gifts—and was evidently stirring up as much question then as now!

Paul was, in effect, saying, "Come on, straighten up! Don't let the gifts of the Holy Spirit turn the Church into chaos! That's why God gives them! Let things be done decently and in order. *Let love rule your hearts* so that the Holy Spirit can have His free will to operate through you with gifts that he's given you!"

Yes, each gift *is* important—how could *anything that God gives us* not be important?

But naturally, Satan, working through our human failings, can mess up the beauty of God's gifts—if we lack love. Have we forgotten Jesus' words? He said that if we love God *and* our fellow man we have fulfilled the law. Building from there on the "1st principles" of Hebrews 6:1-3 we're meant to grow into powerful, loving children of the King!

That's why the current raging discord over the gifts of the Spirit makes me so sad. The very gifts of God that are meant to build up (to edify), and unite the body—(I Corinthians 14:14 and Eph. 4:1-16) are being used by Satan to disrupt and divide it! *But this exact thing was happening in First Century Corinth*— so Paul wrote the great chapter on love right in the middle of his teaching about the gifts. Because *they're spiritual dynamite, powerful and dangerous*—to Satan and his hordes—and to us, if we misunderstand and misuse them!

Still, praise the Lord, God deals with us as individuals in response to our faith, obedience and prayer, as we seek His will. He deals with us with His unchanging love, and as the Giver of all good gifts. He'll instruct us in the use of this dynamite—if we'll let Him.

Millions and millions of people remain to be reached. And *can* be, by the Holy Spirit in cooperation with God's people who, like Paul in First Corinthians, four, recognized that "the Kingdom of God is not in word, but in power."

But they'll be reached by men who believe *all* the

words of Jesus, not just some of them. They'll be reached by men who experience *all* of the New Testament teaching. First Corinthians and elsewhere, and not just the part that fits into our house-of-cards, or our powerless, judgmental doctrines. They will be reached by men who, above all, endeavor to keep Jesus' new commandment we read about in John thirteen: "And so I am giving a new commandment to you now—love each other just as much as I love you. *Your strong love for each other will prove to the world that you are my disciples.*"

They'll be reached by people who understand, like Paul, that the Holy Spirit means to minister through *all* of us, employing His rich spiritual gifts, and especially the gift of love, which "beareth all things, *believeth all things,* hopeth all things, and endureth all things" (I Corinthians 13:7).

The heart-cry of the Old Testament prophet Isaiah was that we should listen *to what the Lord says.* Jesus came with the same heart-cry, urging us to come to the Father through Him like little children—and allow others to do the same. Isaiah pronounced many "woes" on those who stubbornly resist the God of love, mercy and justice. Jesus was frighteningly harsh in His own pronouncement of "woes"—especially toward the stiff-necked, prideful, judgmental religious leaders—and upon *all* who set themselves to disbelieve and reject His own precious Spirit. Over and over, receiving Him like little children, He urged us to be motivated by love, and as willing to forgive others as He has forgiven us. He said emphatically, that each of us must be "born again," to become like babies—to start all over, helpless and innocent.

Why then must we persist in trying to come to Jesus as Rhodes Scholars, Ph.D.s and intellectual giants, damning those who have the audacity to see things differently than we do?

Jesus opened His arms to prostitutes, tax collectors, publicans and sinners—and loved and ministered to them, *even after they had turned their backs on Him and denied Him with curses!* How can we possibly

137

think that Jesus is pleased with us, when we, like Diotrephes in Third John, use "malicious words against our brethren, receive them not, forbid them that would, and even cast them out of the church?" Can't we hear His piercing words in Matthew seven? Hasn't the beam in our own eyes become so great and blinding that we don't even realize *we're like Saul of Tarsus, crippled and helpless, waiting and needing the touch of some humble, Spirit-love-filled disciple?*

This is where I was, just several years ago. I was full of doctrine and self-righteousness, quite sure of my own "status" with God and the spiritual poverty of others—and *almost totally ineffectual* in my communication of God's love to others.

Since my hilltop (or Damascus Road) encounter with the Lord, I've been made aware of my smallness and stupidity, my lack of love. Now I see His greatness and the mind of Christ like I'd never seen it before. The learning and teaching experiences have come in mounting abundance; my family has had miraculous, amazing answers to prayer; and our lives have taken on a first century, Spirit-love-filled dimension.

God has put something precious in our hands as my family have each come to Him in submission, like babes again, and asked for the gift of the Holy Spirit, which He promised every believer on the day of Pentecost.

We asked; He gave.

"If you then, being evil, know how to give good gifts unto your children: how much more shall your Heavenly Father give the Holy Spirit *to them that ask Him?*" (Luke 11:13).

Now we long to share His Good things with others, because the greatest gift of all is in our hearts, "because the love of God is shed abroad in our hearts by the *Holy Ghost* which is given unto us." (Romans 5:5).

30

ROMANS 8:28 IS STILL OPERATIVE

The Church of the New Testament was universal, evangelical and, of course, pentecostal.

The devil has succeeded in getting these three precious thrusts divided—and most major churches today have fragmented and built their organizations around only parts of the truth. Every organization that calls itself Christian has at least part of the truth. But none that I know of has it all nor are they functioning in full First Century power and purity. No one has a corner on all the truth—we all fail in some way or another, because we're fallible.

One church group for instance, has sought doctrinal purity and placed its emphasis there; another has had great pentecostal zeal with an accompanying emphasis on gifts, but with obvious doctrinal weakness; still another may possess great evangelical zeal, but without pentecostal power. And so often in the individual members of each group there is this lack of love, a universal blindness to the action of God's Holy Spirit working in *all* our lives.

I don't think we have to undergo some unruly embarrassing outward display to truly experience the Holy Spirit in our lives and worship. In fact, in I Corinthians fourteen, Paul was *forbidding* any kind of undisciplined emotional display—he was pleading for decency and order, even though the gifts of the Spirit were all operating in that Corinthian fellowship. But many of us have gone to the *other* extreme and said that it is not necessary for these gifts to be operative at all today. Now, somewhere in the middle there is the balance that Paul was preaching about; and if we will only seek the indwelling of the Holy Spirit and let Him lead and guide us, He can be trusted to direct our worship, public and private. What a tremendous difference this would make in the corporate life of the Church—the very body of Jesus—here on earth today!

When I talk about the indwelling of the Spirit, and being submitted to His leading in worship and praise, lots of folks think I'm describing some ecstatic emotional trance, or rolling in the aisles or shouting in some unintelligible noises. I'm *not*. I've never experienced anything of the kind! I'm not criticizing anybody or his tradition; I've just found that God allows us to be ourselves, even as we worship Him.

In Acts eight, we have the story of that dear black Eunuch making his way down to Ethiopia. Down the dusty road, waiting for him, was a young Christian named Philip. Now, because he had the Holy Spirit dwelling in him, Philip was subject to the Spirit's leading; and when that Spirit nudged him and said, "Go over and walk along beside that chariot," Philip quickly "ran over and heard what the Eunuch was reading (from the book of the prophet Isaiah), and asked, 'Do you understand it?'

" 'Of course not,' the man replied. 'How can I when there is no one to instruct me?' And he begged Philip to come up into the chariot and sit with him."

You know the story.

Philip began with the passage the Eunuch was reading, in Isaiah, which spoke of Jesus being led as a sheep to the slaughter. Philip went on from there, using many other scripture references, to tell him about Jesus. The Holy Spirit was working powerfully in that chariot—with just two men—that, as they approached some small lake, the Ethiopian asked if he could be baptized *right then!* I'm sure there was emotion in that request, and in Philip's response; but the

Spirit was gently guiding and prompting them. Philip asked his companion if he believed in Jesus with all his heart—and the Eunuch repied, "I believe that Jesus is the Son of God."

That was enough! The chariot halted, the two men went down into the water, and a spiritual wedding ceremony took place on the spot! How glorious!

But what happened to Philip and what happened to the Ethiopian then? "The Spirit of the Lord caught away Philip, and the Eunuch never saw him again." Yet, the Eunuch went "on his way rejoicing!"

I don't know what that means to you, but "rejoicing" indicates to me that this new-born Christian was having a wonderful time praising our Lord!

That same Holy Spirit is working in the world today. When that black Eunuch finally arrived in Ethiopia, *he was* the Church in Ethiopia. And today, 2000 years later, the official religion in Ethiopia is Christian!

Can the Holy Spirit be trusted to teach and guide a man into *all* truth? Can the Holy Spirit take care of us as individual believers and disciples of Christ? Can I trust Him to show you *your* imperfections as He shows me mine? I believe we can trust in the same God who took care of both Philip and the Eunuch as they parted!

Only God can bring any of us into a proper understanding of His will, but one thing is for sure—Romans 8:28 is still operative today: "And we know that *all things work together for good* to them that love God, to them who are called according to His purpose."

Praise Jesus!

I'm about to "go on my way rejoicing"!

31

ME AND BALAAM'S ASS

God can communicate through anybody He chooses, *with or without the conscious knowledge* of the vessel being used; if He could do it with stones, He can surely use people who are straining and desiring to do His will and speak His thoughts! Jesus indicated in Luke 20:40 that God could speak through *rocks* if He wanted to!

I have had correspondence and conversation with church people who have indicated to me their conviction that anyone who actually has received either the Holy Spirit or any of the charismatic gifts, and through whom the Holy Spirit may have spoken or worked in any form and at any time, should be immediately thought of as an apostle or prophet. These brothers of mine seem to feel that if the Spirit of God has actually filled and inspired and motivated a person to deliver some specific word from the Lord, that henceforth most, if not all, of that person's future utterances should be dutifully recorded and added to the Bible!

Of course the inference is plain—it is that such "charismatic" people are *not* led by the Spirit of God, that God is *not* working in His First Century pattern today.

I've actually been asked, "which of your writings, Mr. Boone, is 'inspired?' " I suppose you can almost hear the tone of the question—and assess its sincerity.

If all "inspired" utterances were to have been recorded, I have to ask: Where is the Epistle of Balaam's ass?

In Numbers Twenty-Two, you may recall, the Lord spoke twice through an ass. Part of the reason was that the ass recognized the angel of the Lord, while the prophet didn't. But this dumb animal *actually delivered messages from God!*

In this instance, there was a specific need, a particular message to be delivered, and the ass was the only willing messenger around. There are those of us who believe that God still will motivate willing *people* by His sovereign Spirit, to speak truth. We're happy to be used in the same capacity as that dumb ass, if the Lord finds us worthy. What a happy privilege!

If the Lord says something through a yielded person today, there's no need to add that message to the Scripture. God has said what He wants said in the Bible; if a man could memorize the whole Bible, and *understand* it perfectly, he'd be ready for anything that came up. But few people who ever lived have been intellectually capable of even the first part of that recipe, much less the second. Therefore, if we really want to do the will of the Lord in *all* things, including the complex or spur-of-the-moment things, we become dependent on the Holy Spirit, as God wants us to be. We must ask Him to do for us what He did for Balaam, Jesus' disciples and so many others—and that is, to open our eyes!

Open our eyes, not to new revelation, new scriptures —but to truth that's been there staring at us all along! Or to the Lord's solution to an immediate problem that we have.

Both Old and New Testaments abound with examples of what I'm saying. The New Testament writers allude to scriptures and prophets that God *didn't* preserve for us today. Joshua and Samuel both speak of the "book of Jasher"—where is it? Surely God inspired it, and its writer, for a time and need that has now passed. Some revelations have been temporary, even momentary—others permanent. Are we to discredit the temporary, momentary insights that God has been giving to His saints through the intervening centuries?

In Second Kings Twenty-Two, eighteen-year-old King Josiah rediscovered the book of the law of God, after it had gathered dust for years, hidden away and ignored. The truth hadn't changed, or disappeared from the earth, but men, even the King and his religious leaders, had grown satisfied with their own understanding and did not continually seek *God's* guidance. So the Lord, in His mercy, refocused the attention of His people, through an eighteen-year-old servant, on His Word and His will. *HE* opened *their* eyes!

We will *always* need this acting of His Spirit. Luke records for us in Chapter Twenty-Four two examples of Jesus doing this. The first is the episode which occurred with two of Jesus' followers who were walking to the village of Emmaus, seven miles out of Jerusalem. Jesus joined them, but they didn't recognize Him, for God kept them from it. They were in a deep discussion and Jesus got them to tell Him about it. Of course it concerned Jesus' death, His crucifixion at the hand of the Roman government.

But they went on to explain about Jesus' bodily disappearance, and expressed sorrow at the fact that His body was missing. "Then Jesus said to them, 'You are such foolish, foolish people! You find it so hard to believe all that the prophets wrote in the Scriptures! Wasn't it clearly predicted by the prophets that the Messiah would have to suffer all these things before entering His time of glory?'

"Then Jesus quoted them passage after passage from the writing of the prophets, beginning with the book of Genesis and going right on through the Scriptures, explaining what the passages meant and what they said about Himself.

"By this time they were nearing Emmaus and the end of their journey. Jesus would have gone on, but they begged Him to stay the night with them, as it was getting late. So he went home with them. As they sat down to eat, He asked God's blessing on the food and then took a small loaf of bread and broke it and was passed over to them, when suddenly—it was as though *their eyes were opened*—they recognized Him! And at that moment He disappeared!" (Verses 25-31, itals. author's.)

These followers of Jesus *had* the scriptures, they *knew* them, they had concepts about them—but they didn't *understand* them—until Jesus did His Divine thing!

Still later in that same chapter, we read of the two from Emmaus heading back to Jerusalem within the hour to tell the eleven disciples and the other followers of Jesus what had happened. "And just as they were telling about it, Jesus Himself was suddenly standing there among all of them, and greeted them. But the whole group was terribly frightened, thinking they were seeing a ghost!

" 'Why are you frightened?' he asked. 'Why do you doubt that it is really I?' " (Verses 36-38). At that point Jesus shows them His hands and feet. He invited them to touch Him stating that ghosts don't have bodies, as He did!

"Still they stood there undecided, filled with joy and doubt.

"Then He asked them, 'Do you have anything here to eat?'

"They gave Him a piece of broiled fish, and He ate it as they watched!

"Then He said, 'When I was with you before, don't you remember my telling you that everything written about Me by Moses and the prophets and in the Psalms must all come true?' *Then He opened their minds to understand at last* these many Scriptures!" (Verses 41-45).

Even the words from Jesus' lips and the fantastic miracles from His hands were not sufficient to convince many, including the religious experts of His earthly time! He said, "If they hear not Moses and the prophets, neither will they be persuaded, though one rose from the dead" (Luke 16:31). He also said, "No man can come to Me, *except the Father which sent Me draw him*"! (John 6:44).

145

There must be an interaction between the revealed Word and the Revealer of Truth. Though we all have access to the Scripture which was inspired by the Holy Spirit, we still must cry out to that same Spirit to inspire our understanding, to open our eyes spiritually!

He is not confined to the printed page! The Bible demonstrates to me so vividly that God wants His Spirit to be a continuing dynamic force in us. Though we have the Scriptures, which are able to furnish us into perfection, yet He knows our imperfections and ragged intellects, and hovers near the believer to *personally* guide and protect and caution. He'll do it, Himself, in Person. Doesn't Jesus say "*I am with you always, even to the end of the world*"!?

Surely God will do for us what He did for His other followers. He will do for us what He did, for example, for Paul. Here was a man, filled with the Spirit and hearing the voice of God directly; and yet God chose Agabus (Acts 21) to prophesy to Paul on one occasion, and his nephew to warn him on another (Acts 23:16). Why? Because it pleased Him, and because He wants the Body of Christ to interact, its members to be interdependent and to *minister to each other*, infused, led and built up by the living Spirit! This is what the Bible is all about. What folly for any of us to so depend on his own understanding of the perfect Scriptures that he doesn't hear God's Spirit speaking to him through other Christians!

This doesn't take away in any way from the "all-sufficiency of the Scriptures"! It simply points up *our insufficiency!*

We are meant to read the Scriptures and interpret them, but not only that, we're to launch from the Word (and with it) into a dynamic, emotional, challenging, unpredictable, victorious and continually eye-opening relationship with our Bridegroom, the living-ever-present Jesus!

Sometimes we don't interpret His Word the same as other individual believers; sometimes we respond to it in different ways. But God still chooses to use us and speak to and through us anyway! In spite of all the imperfections and human filth in each of us. All I can say is, "Praise His glorious Name!"

If God had chosen to speak only through perfect vessels, we wouldn't have much Bible today, would we?

Only Jesus then could have spoken; and we wouldn't have even had the testimony of Balaam's ass—much less Peter, Paul, James and John. I am not claiming that the Holy Spirit has "inspired" this book in the way He inspired the Scriptures to be written (a man would have to be mighty foolish to claim that!). But I do claim the fact that He has aided in my understanding the Scriptures to a far greater degree than ever before. He has opened my eyes and my understanding. No longer do I try to muddle through on my own.

Jesus promised the guidance of the Holy Spirit. "When the Father sends the Comforter instead of me—and by the Comforter I mean the Holy Spirit— He will teach you much, as well as remind you of everything I myself have told you" (John 14:26). It is a beautiful thing; He's so real, so near; and this precious Spirit has brought my family and me closer to God.

This is the greatest testimony of all—that it is truly the work of God—*we are changed people.*

32

THE BAPTISM OF THE HOLY SPIRIT
WHY, WHO, HOW—AND THEN WHAT?

"And He said unto them, he that hath ears to hear, let him hear.

"Unto you it is given to know the mystery of the Kingdom of God: but unto them that are without, all these things are done in parables:

That seeing they may see and not perceive; and *hearing they may hear and not understand;* lest at any time they should be converted, and their sins should be forgiven them" (Jesus in Mark 4:9, 11, 12).

But God hath chosen the foolish things of the world to confound the wise; and God hath chosen the weak things of the world to confound the things which are mighty;

And base things of the world, *and things which are despised, hath God chosen,* yea, and things which are not, to bring to nought things that are:

"That no flesh should glory in His presence." (Paul, in I Corinthians 1:27-29).

"But we speak the wisdom of God in a mystery, even the hidden wisdom, which God ordained before the world unto our glory:

"Which none of the princes of this world knew: *for had they known it, they would not have crucified the Lord of glory.*

"But as it is written, Eye hath Not seen, *nor ear heard,* neither have entered into the heart of man, the things which God hath prepared for them that love Him.

"But God hath revealed them unto us by His Spirit: for the Spirit searcheth all things, yea, the deep things of God." (Paul, in I Corinthians 2:7-10).

"For he that speaketh in an unknown tongue *speaketh not unto men,* but unto God; for no man understands him; however, *in the spirit he speaketh mysteries*." (I Corinthians 14:2).

My friend, if you've stayed with me this far, through all my ramblings and "ass-type" brayings, I believe the Lord is about to reward you. Maybe it's been a real test of your faith to wade through this wilderness with me—but we come now to a clearing, an oasis, where the pure refreshing water of the Holy Spirit is waiting for you.

We're on Holy ground; I know it.

Look back over those scriptures. They're not my words; they were spoken and revealed by Jesus himself.

He's talking about a mystery—a secret—an ever unfolding, relentless, minutely detailed but hidden plan of God. And though He came to reveal it, and to effectively accomplish it, He *purposely* clouded it and veiled it enough that not everyone could understand it!

Why?

Doesn't He want everyone to be saved? Of course He does.

But I see at least two powerful reasons for cloaking His profound truths in mystery and "foolishness."

Paul gives us a chilling glimpse at one of the reasons: God hides His divine plan from natural man so that Satan and his demonic legions can't thwart it! If they'd *known* that crucifying Jesus was sealing their own doom, they wouldn't have done it. They would be protecting Him to this day, though He blistered and bruised their heads these last 2000 years!

And right now, when they can see what you and I plan to do in God's Kingdom and what God *wants* us to do, they scramble like crazy to throw up road blocks and prevent it, if they can.

So the Lord continues to reveal truth to believers by

His spirit—and to leave it opaque and impenetrable, strangely vague to natural man, and even to "carnal," fleshly Christians. He does that for our sakes, and the Gospel's.

Oh, the simple salvation message can be understood by even a child (though many theologians still don't see it)—but the deeper things, the Kingdom-building, Satan-blinding things are whispered supernaturally to Spirit-filled sons of God.

God has His reasons.

And one of them, the second that I see, is that the *Almighty God demands faith!* Thundering, reverberating from the garden of Eden, fanned by the flaming sword of the Cherubims who guard the Tree of Life, echoing through the ruins of the Tower of Babel, lashing the floods under Noah's ark, shattering the Red Sea and wasting Pharaoh's armies, binding the people of Israel and destroying thousands of disbelievers in a moment of time, devastating Babylon and Egypt, Persia, Greece and Rome, cascading over the mountains of man's intellect and achievement; piercing the council-rooms of Moscow, Peking, London and Washington, and shaking the earth in ever-increasing crescendos, through all of the days of man on this earth until this very second, the mighty voice of God resounds:

I WILL BE BELIEVED!

I WILL BE BELIEVED!

I WILL BE BELIEVED!

No man will come to God through his intellect, by understanding and perceiving His way. In the beginning, He ordered "you shall not eat of the tree of knowledge; believe me or die!"

Adam tried to approach God-status through knowledge—and he died.

Simply because he refused to just believe God, to accept Him at His Word, to obey a loving Father's commands—even though the reasons were hidden—man cut himself off from God. He chose to let his brain rule his spirit, and so his spirit perished.

But Abraham! *"He believed in the Lord, and He*

counted it to him for righteousness." (Genesis 15)

Believed what?

Some rational, practical preachment? Some theologically, intellectually reasonable doctrinal truth?

NO—Abraham believed in the Lord who had just told him preposterous, incredible things about his descendants being numbered like the stars and blessing the whole earth—*and then ordered him to be circumcised* at age ninety-nine!

I WILL BE BELIEVED!

And Abraham believed God, and was lifted to a supernatural level of life.

He became God's partner in blessing the whole world. Rather incredible isn't it?

Hallelujah!

We've talked several times in these pages about "the scriptural pattern"; well, when you read again the 11th chapter of Hebrews, you really get a fast, sharp overview of God's scriptural "pattern." Over and over, from Genesis to Revelation, our Lord has demanded that His believing children demonstrate their faith in the most unimaginable, irrational ways. We were *created* for this: to share in a fantastic partnership with God, being led by His Spirit to ever-greater adventure and dominion—but at the same time, being humbled and tested like children, so that our egos and intellects remain in subjection to our spirits . . . and so that our spirits stay subject to His.

Oh, friend, I could write a whole book about just this principle—but somebody beat me to it. It's called the Bible.

Hear God say it: "But without faith (substance of things *hoped for,* evidence of things *not seen*) it is impossible to please Him: for he that cometh to God must *believe that He is,* and that He is a rewarder of them that diligently seek Him (Hebrews 11:1 and 6)"! I used to think this was a one-time proposition; now I see that God intends it to be a continuing process.

I WILL BE BELIEVED!

Again: "And these signs shall follow *them that believe;* in my name shall they cast out devils; they shall·

151

speak with new tongues; they shall take up serpents; and if they drink any deadly thing, it shall not hurt them; they shall lay hands on the sick, and they shall recover.

"And they went forth, and preached everywhere, *the Lord working with them,* and confirming the word with signs following" (Mark 16:18 and 20).

I WILL BE BELIEVED!

God wants partners—junior associates in His business! And His business is reclaiming the earth and everything in it. He created this whole globe for you and me, and meant for us to run it completely, guided by His Spirit. But we let the thief Satan take it, and pervert and ruin it. God wants it back—and he wants His sons and daughters to be the instruments of its reclamation, regaining dominion the same way it was lost, in *personal confrontation with Satan!*

And as we lost our inheritance through *un*belief, God intends us to regain it one way: through BELIEF!

What's all this got to do with the baptism in the Holy Spirit?

Everything!

God wanted personal relationship with all His children; *but relationship has been lost in religion.*

It's become so easy to melt into a crowd, to slip into a nice comfortable doctrine, to place membership with a respectable group—and proceed to do the "right things" with the "right people" at the "right times," and *never meet the Lord!*

This has been the devil's greatest, most tragic theft: a masterful bit of sleight-of-hand by which he traded man's ritual, doctrine, theology, pomp, intrigue, self-righteousness and all the other fancy ingredients of "religion" for his spiritual birthright—relationship and partnership with God.

It's like what Jacob did to Esau in Genesis 27. The devil has concocted an elaborate experience that "*feels* like religion, and *looks* and *smells* like religion, and *feeds* a spiritual hunger like religion—surely this must be the genuine article!" And there are many good things in most Christian denominations.

152

One vital ingredient is missing. *Power*.

"But as many as received Him, to them gave He power to become the *sons of God* even to them that *believe* on His name" (John 1:12).

There's that word again: BELIEVE. And now it's linked with another word: POWER. Jesus promised power in Acts 1:8, "But you shall receive power, after the Holy Ghost is come upon you"! All these disciples had been baptized in water (vs. 5), but now Jesus wanted to baptize them with His own promised Holy Spirit, that they might have supernatural endowment to be His witnesses throughout the earth.

See, water baptism is something *you and I* do; Spirit baptism is something only *Jesus* can do (John 1:33). A partnership arrangement again—get it?

I earnestly believe there are millions of saved people on this earth right now who have no idea of how to act like children of God. I've been there! For most of my life I was like the elder brother of the prodigal son, just hangin' around and not gettin' into too much trouble— and accomplishing zero—or close to it.

Now I identify with the prodigal son himself, and am very aware of my own failures. And I see that it's not till a man becomes empty and helpless and painfully close to complete defeat, till he is willing to return to his father's house and be a servant—*willing to serve his elder brother,* if need be, for the rest of his life—that he finds the Lord Himself running to meet him, kissing him with compassion, throwing a robe (Isaiah 61:3 and 10) of praise over him, placing a ring of authority (Ephesians 1:13, 14) on his hand, and preparing his feet to run with the Good News (Ephesians 6:15)!

May I humbly suggest to you that this is the real "why" of the baptism in the Holy Spirit: our Father wants to give every one of His children *power* to serve, to witness, and to overcome the enemy.

Jesus didn't confront the enemy, Satan, until He Himself was baptized with water and the Spirit (Matthew 3 and 4)—and then He was led *by the Spirit* into the wilderness to overcome Satan, and into the world to serve. Is it any wonder that so many of our religious efforts are stifled and ineffectual when we try to serve without Jesus' own power-source? Is it any wonder that Jesus expressly commanded His disciples to "wait for the promise of the Father" before hey went out to serve? "For John truly baptized with water; but you shall be baptized with the Holy Ghost not many days hence" (Acts 1:4, 5).

Of course, you can be saved without that promised gift; and the disciples could have been marvelous preachers and personal workers without it, too. After all, they were graduates of Jesus' own seminary; they had their doctrine straight; they were eye-witnesses to enough sermon material for many lifetimes; and they had the desire.

But Jesus wanted them to have more than all that— He wanted to add to these *natural* abilities His own *supernatural* power! And He wants to do it for you and me today!

As the age comes to a close, as the prophecies are all being fulfilled, as the final showdown with Satan comes upon us and Jesus is preparing His bride for His own appearance, He wants to equip us with mighty weapons "to the pulling down of strongholds" (II Corinthians 10:4). He wants His virgins to be wise and to have the oil of the Holy Spirit in their vessels (Matthew 25).

Over and over, the New Testament writers stressed the need for disciples to have the Lord's own mighty power working in us, equipping us for service, (Philemon 2:12 and 13, Ephesians 4:7-13 and 6:10-18, II Thessalonians 1:11 and 12, and more). "He therefore that *ministereth to you the Spirit, and worketh miracles among you,* doeth he it by the works of the law, or by the hearing of faith?

"Even as Abraham believed God, and it was accounted to him for righteousness. Know ye therefore that they which are of faith, the same are the children of Abraham" (Galatians 3:5-7).

I WILL BE BELIEVED!

If you're not convinced of your need for this baptism with the Holy Spirit, you might as well put this book aside now. But if you see the "Why"—the rest is easy.

Next comes "who?"

Peter answered that for all time in the very first sermon on Pentecost: "For the promise is unto *you* and to your children, and to all that are afar off, *even* as many as the Lord our God shall call" (Acts 2:38, 39).

The gift of the Holy Spirit is for every Christian, every believer.

For you.

What about the "how"?

There are a lot of wonderful books on that, but the basic answer is so simple: *You ask,* and *you receive.*

"If you then, being evil, know how to give good gifts unto your children: how much more shall your heavenly Father give the Holy Spirit to them that *ask* Him?" Everyone that hungers and thirsts after righteousness "shall be filled" (Luke 11:13 and Matthew 5:6).

So ask Him, humbly and earnestly, as a child asks his parent.

And then receive: Jesus, in John 20:22, gave His disciples a foretaste and an admonition, when He breathed on them and said "*Receive ye* the Holy Ghost." Paul asked the Ephesian disciples in Acts 19, "have you *received* the Holy Ghost since you believed?" And then he asked the Galatians, "Received you the Spirit by the works of the law (doctrine), or by the hearing of faith?" (Galatians 3:2).

You make it sound so simple, Boone. Is it really that easy?

Yes, it is, if you believe the Lord Jesus. Because it's up to Him to baptize you (John 1:33), and up to you to *ask,* and to *believe* that He'll do what He says! He is the "rewarder of them that diligently seek Him," and the giver of "living water" (John 7:38 and 39).

"Okay," you say, "I've done that; I've asked, and I believe that I've received—but I haven't had that manifestation I've heard so much about, that 'prayer language' that 'speaking in tongues'. What's wrong? Doesn't He want me to have that, too?"

Yes, He does. Your parents wanted you to have the gift of speaking English, too. How did you receive that?

155

Didn't you begin to act as if you already had that gift? Didn't you start talking, even while you were lying in your crib? Didn't you lift your arms to your folks and start telling them you loved them, and wanted them to pick you up, and to love and feed you—even though you hadn't learned the words? And didn't they get the message? Didn't they respond? What if you and your parents had waited until you could put whole intelligent sentences together, and converse like adults?

You didn't do that. You began to speak, to express your love and your needs—and the understanding and fluency of your language came later. You *received* your gift of language like the trusting, unashamed baby that you were!

Jesus told the religious leaders of His day, *"Out of the mouths of babes and sucklings* (nursing infants) *God has perfected praise"* (Matthew 21:16). The intellectual giants of Jesus' time had no answer for that; they don't today.

Listen again to Jesus, as He talks intimately with His Father (Matthew 11), "I thank thee, O Father, Lord of heaven and earth, because *thou has hid these things from the wise and prudent, and has revealed them unto babes"!*

And Paul, in the great 13th Chapter of 1st Corinthians, on tongues, "When I was a child, I spoke as a child"! I used to misapply this scripture to establish that tongues were childish (they are, in the best spiritual sense), and that mature men shouldn't expect that experience. But that's not Paul's meaning at all. Because, by his own admission, (verse 18 of the next chapter, he was still exercising that supremely "childlike" gift more than anybody! His point was that not until he became a completed, perfected *man* (Ephesians 4:13)—until the whole body of Christ is perfected into the mature fulness of Jesus Himself—would these "childish" gifts be rendered unnecessary. Until then (and it hasn't happened yet), the gangly adolescent *im*perfect church would still be seeing "through a glass darkly," and would need all the ministry and help of the Holy Spirit it could get!

So, unless you consider yourself more mature than the apostle Paul—be willing to "speak like a child," *ask* and *receive* the Holy Spirit, "desire spiritual gifts" and dare to be childlike in your response to God the Father, who reveals His truth most perfectly "unto babes."

Ask Jesus to baptize you, fill you, with His Spirit, and to enable you to praise him like a spiritual baby, being "edified" or built up in your inner being (I Cor. 14:4). Ask the Holy Spirit to help you "speak mysteries" to God (vs. 2) and to gradually reveal the "hidden things," the mysterious wisdom of this our Spirit (I Corinthains 2:7-10) to *you*—as you search His Word and "stir up the gift that is in you." Ask him to increase your faith as you dare to exercise your new spiritual muscles.

He'll do it!

Finally,—"and then what?"

Above all else, having received the Holy Spirit and one or another of His gifts, don't stay a baby! Allow Him to help you "grow up"! Ask Him to show you how to minister to others, how to understand His word, how to cultivate and practice the other gifts, how to praise and serve Him better and better—how to "become children of God" (John 1:12).

Dig into the Word; it'll come alive. "Study to show thyself approved unto God, a *workman* that needeth not to be ashamed, rightly dividing the word of truth" (II Timothy 2:15). Make time for this fantastic adventure of discovery!

Pray all the time, with your spirit *and* with your understanding! They go together (I Corinthians 14:15). Ask God to enrich your understanding through your prayer life, and to begin to give you the "hidden manna" (Revelation 2:17), to reveal to you of His wisdom, His mysteries by His Spirit (I Corinthians 2)— and He will!

Ask Him for power to "tread on scorpions," and to "bruise the head of the serpent," to break and bind the power of the enemy in your life and in the lives of others. He'll do it! Exercise your new spiritual muscles, and dare to do battle, equipped with all His mighty armor—Ephesians 6:10-18.

Get into regular, concentrated fellowship with other Spirit-filled believers and rejoice at what God's doing in *their* lives; be part of a "body ministry" to a sick society around you, and gain strength from serving shoulder to shoulder with your brothers and sisters. We need each other!

I could go on and on; but really, it's all in the precious black Book you have near you. It's not for me to try to paraphrase what the Lord has already given you so abundantly. Read it eagerly; talk to Him constantly; *do* what He tells you and mix faith with your hearing. What a life! What a Saviour! What a victorious destiny, and it's already begun—we're *in* it, we're in Him, and He is in us! Jesus the Christ, "the same yesterday, and today, and for ever" (Hebrews 13:8) is in us, and as the beloved John promised, "Greater is He that is in you than he that is in the world" (I John 4:4)

To our Jesus be the praise, and the honor, and the glory—for ever, starting now!

"For as you know him better he will give you, *through his great power, everything you need* for living a truly good life: he even shares his own glory and his own goodness with us!"

And by that same mighty power he has given us all the other rich and wonderful blessings he promised; for instance, the promise to save us from the lust and rottenness all around us, and to give us his own character.

But to obtain these gifts, you need more than faith; you must also work hard to be good, and even that is not enough. For then you must learn *to know God better and discover what he wants you to do.*

Next, learn to put aside your own desire so that you will become patient and godly, gladly letting God have his way with you. This will make possible the next step, which is for you to enjoy other people and to like them, and finally you will grow to love them deeply. The more you go on in this way, the more you will

158

grow strong spiritually and become fruitful and useful to our Lord Jesus Christ.

But anyone who fails to go after these additions to faith is *blind indeed,* or at least very shortsighted, and has forgotten that God delivered him from the old life of sin so that now he can live a strong, good life for the Lord.

So, dear brother, work hard to prove that you really are among those God has called and chosen, and then you will never stumble or fall away. "And God will open wide the gates of heaven for you to enter into the eternal kingdom of our Lord and Savior Jesus Christ" (II Peter 1:3-11, *Living Bible*).

Thank you, brother Peter.

And thank you, Jesus, for showing me that I *am* to be my brother's keeper.